Personal and Social Education
For Primary Schools
Through Circle-Time

Mollie Curry and Carolyn Bromfield

A NASEN Publication

Published in 1994
Reprinted in 1995
© Mollie Curry and Carolyn Bromfield

ISBN 0 906730 62 7

Published by NASEN Enterprises Ltd.
NASEN Enterprises is a company limited by guarantee, registered in England and Wales.
Company No. 2637438

Further copies of this book and details of NASEN's many other publications may be obtained from the Publications Department at its registered office:
NASEN House, 4/5 Amber Business Village, Amber Close, Amington, Tamworth, Staffs. B77 4RP
Telephone: 01827 311500   Fax: 01827 313005

Cover Design by Pam Crewe.
Typeset in Helvetica Narrow and printed in the United Kingdom by J. H. Brookes Ltd., Stoke-on-Trent.

PERSONAL AND SOCIAL EDUCATION IN PRIMARY SCHOOLS THROUGH CIRCLE-TIME

Contents

PERSONAL AND SOCIAL EDUCATION IN PRIMARY SCHOOLS THROUGH CIRCLE-TIME

Foreword

Circle-time is one of a family of approaches which aims to help mobilise the power of the group experience for the benefit of the individual children in a class. The title stresses the common form of working while sitting in a circle which, as the introduction to this book makes clear, signals that:

> '.....everyone is equal, everyone can be seen and heard, people can make eye contact, they can speak to one another more easily, there are no barriers such as tables or desks and everyone feels part of the group.'

To make everyone feel part of the group is an important part of the work of Mollie Curry and Carolyn Bromfield as they provide support for pupils who find it difficult to fit into the daily life of a class. This book makes these ideas available to a larger audience of primary teachers and contains a wide range of suggestions as to how the approach may be used in implementing a PSE programme for primary schools.

The book is a welcome addition to the provision at this phase of education and the authors give detailed guidance on material they have found helpful and give many examples of ways in which material can be used to explore themes of personal and social relevance.

Teachers new to the approach will find much to give them confidence in starting off this work with their classes. The structured plans give clear guidance to teachers as to how to construct a well balanced session which involves not just using activities which the children find enjoyable and stimulating but also 'conferencing' these activities when completed in order that the activity might be reflected on and the learning extracted. It is this process which I would encourage people using this work to adopt.

Reflect on the work contained in this book as you use it. As your confidence grows, develop your own ideas and those of your class to construct Circle-time sessions. Above all let the spirit of respect for the individual person and of co-operation between all spread out from your Circle-time sessions so that it permeates your whole classroom practice and eventually the life of the school. This book is a starting point on this journey.

Dr. John Thacker
University of Exeter

PERSONAL AND SOCIAL EDUCATION IN PRIMARY SCHOOLS THROUGH CIRCLE-TIME

Introduction

This book aims to introduce teachers in primary schools to Circle-time and provide them with some practical examples. Circle-time covers the speaking and listening Attainment Targets in the National Curriculum, and provides the school with a vehicle for delivering its Pastoral Curriculum. Through Circle-time activities children can develop social skills, acquire interpersonal relationship skills, increase awareness of their feelings and become more responsible for their behaviour.

Circle-time:

- injects the 'feel good' factor;

- raises self-esteem;

- improves listening skills;

- facilitates working together co-operatively;

- increases insight and awareness;

- teaches social skills;

- builds confidence;

- promotes effective communication;

- enhances friendships;

- provides conflict resolution strategies;

- encourages problem solving solutions;

- offers understanding;

- makes children more sensitive to one another;

- explores feelings;

- is fun !

We are grateful to the teachers who have used the materials, also to the children who are always enthusiastic and have helped us to 'fine tune' the ideas. This book has been compiled in response to a demand from teachers to provide a comprehensive resource bank. The themes and lesson plans are free standing and can be interchanged and used flexibly according to individual needs.

We hope you enjoy this book and find the ideas useful and helpful.

Mollie Curry and Carolyn Bromfield.

WHAT CHILDREN SAY ABOUT CIRCLE-TIME

- 'I really like Special Person when Miss gets your name out of the box. You don't know who it's going to be.'
- 'Circle-time makes me happy.'
- 'We can learn things and know what to do when something goes wrong.'
- 'Listening to other people - it's interesting.'
- 'I like showing things in Circle-time because everybody gets a good look.'
- 'The look on the special person's face.'
- 'I like talking about different things, about friends and what to do if they don't like me.'
- 'I like the Warm Fuzzy story and hate the Cold Pricklies.'
- 'The games are great fun and nobody loses.'
- 'Learning new things about people is interesting.'
- 'I'm getting much better at talking to people I don't know well.'
- 'I like talking in twos as someone really listens to me.'
- 'Being 'special person' made me feel important and I liked my new name.'
- 'I like sharing things and making new friends.'
- 'Circle-time has helped me sort out playground problems.'
- 'Circle-time – it's great !'

CHAPTER 1 – CIRCLE-TIME : A DESCRIPTION

'Circle-time' is a way of supporting children and enhancing self-esteem, of making a safe environment in which to take risks, to explore feelings, to discuss conflicts in a non-blaming, non-punitive way and a process that encourages children to believe that they are worthwhile people.

It is a time to foster a caring group feeling where each member is valued and valuable, where each child gets a chance to speak and more importantly a chance to be listened to. Circle-time is a time for children to discover more about themselves, their strengths, feelings, preferences, as well as discovering more about their peers. It is accomplished by affirming the positive attributes of self and others. It is a time when children find out more about themselves, what they are capable of and how they relate to one another.

There are lots of serious, lively, discussions where feelings are discovered, explored and accepted. Children come to realise that if they understand themselves it will help them to understand others better. The value of co-operation and friendship is examined and emphasised using practical activities so that children (and the teacher) are involved in experiential learning.

The aims of Circle-time

Circle-time is aimed at developing the unique potential of each individual, of looking at their social and emotional growth and nurturing this within a caring group environment. Circle-time provides the person-centred setting that allows for the development of communication systems built on respect for every person in which healthy positive relationships can flourish.

Children need to acquire the necessary social skills to enable them to live and work together in a harmonious atmosphere. Many children seem to acquire these skills naturally but some children come to school without them, which can lead to inappropriate interactions with the people they meet. This effects their work and can affect the academic progress of a whole class. Social skills can be taught to children and practised in the safety of Circle-time. Research demonstrates that learning is achieved most productively in groups where people can interact and reflect on mutual experiences.

The National Curriculum

OFSTED (The Office For Standards in Education), in an attempt to reach a consensus on moral, spiritual, social and cultural development, has produced a discussion paper. Recent events have brought to the forefront questions of morality and children's behaviour and it is hoped that the document will facilitate discussion. There is a need for some agreement about what is provided in the Pastoral Curriculum and the criteria to be used in school inspections. OFSTED have identified two main areas for development:

the quality of relationships;

the importance of academic achievement to aid personal growth.

Personal and Social Education (PSE) development is central to the National Curriculum and all aspects of a school's PSE curriculum can be addressed through Circle-time.

'....the personal and social development of pupils is a major aim of education; personal and social education being the means by which this aim is achieved.'

NCC Curriculum Guidance No. 3. (1990)

At all levels Circle-time covers many of the components of English Attainment Target 1 in speaking and listening. These include taking turns, knowing when to stop talking and wait for another's response and listening attentively in a group situation. Circle-time enables children to participate as listeners and speakers and facilitates the whole process of communication.

The history of groupwork

Groups have provided the setting for the creation of personal change for thousands of years. In the form of families and all sorts of organisations people have come together to try to create change within their own behaviour and feelings. One of the earliest origins of groupwork is found in the work of Jacob Moreno in Vienna from 1908 onwards. Moreno developed a variety of activities with children meeting in the parks of Vienna after school hours and his methods evolved into the range of techniques now known as psychodrama. Moreno believed that people could find solutions to their problems, not by dwelling in the past but by portraying the issues in a here and now manner. He devised an enormous variety of structured 'warm-up' exercises to facilitate expression and many of these were subsequently reinvented by the encounter leaders of the sixties.

Moreno subsequently moved to America and it was from there that the most frequently identified origin of group work took place. This was the invention of the T-group by Kurt Lewin and others. T-groups arose at a training programme in 1946. It lays great stress on discussion of the 'here and now' behaviour of the group, mutual sharing of perceptions and a participating role of the group leader.

Work in schools developed at a slower pace but when personal and social education was highlighted as being an important part of the curriculum, it was left to form tutors in secondary schools to play a key role in delivering this subject. Subsequently a number of personal and social education (PSE) curricula were developed for use in the secondary school which included interpersonal problem solving, study skills development, social skills training and behavioural self management. At that time, little had been done in the primary system. One person who was also concerned over the lack of pastoral care in primary schools was John Thacker. He directed an interesting project in association with Leslie Button at the School of Education, Exeter University which investigated developmental groupwork in junior and middle schools.

Circle-time itself has developed from similar work and from the 'Quality Circles' approach used by industry.

Getting started

As you would expect from the title, the work is done with children and adults sitting in circles; either on chairs or on the floor. This has the advantage of making sure everyone is equal: everyone can be seen and heard; people can make eye-contact; they can speak to one another more easily; there are no barriers, such as tables or desks, and everyone feels part of the group. There is also the advantage that it reduces distracting behaviour such as chatting, fiddling and so forth, as everyone in the group can see one another and the teacher is able to 'pick up' on these behaviours quickly.

Circle-time is started by inviting everyone in the room (including the adults), to join the circle and sit where they like, with the understanding that they are responsible for their own behaviour and they do not have the right to spoil anyone else's enjoyment. Splitting unlikely pairings, or encouraging children to work with others who they would not normally choose can be accomplished in a painless, non-controlling way by playing any one of numerous mixing games that get people moving round the circle. (see chapter 4 on page 38).

The format

The structure of Circle-time will vary considerably according to the age of the children, their experiences of working together as a group and other similar variables. The ideal size of the group is about 20. Numbers that go over 30 are more difficult to manage, and care in the planning is important to minimise waiting and listening for classes of this size. To ensure that everyone has a fair amount of time in the activities an increased use of pairs and triads is advisable. The frequency and duration of Circle-time is governed by varying levels of concentration, and the constraints of the curriculum. Some teachers have found greater success by having shorter Circle-times, more frequently than a longer session, when listening skills may be stretched, leading to boredom and off task behaviour. Young children will need short sessions with not too much sitting and listening - more participation. Older children are able to contribute to the planning and lead their own circles on agreed topics. In this case it is helpful to have a Circle-time board or book including an agenda sheet that can be added to by anyone in the class for inclusion in the next Circle-time. This is the beauty of Circle-time - the fact that it is flexible and can be designed to suit the needs of your class.

Most circles will include one or two games, a 'round', an activity, and special person , but as previously stated, they can be any combination of these elements. To make it simpler for teachers to use this book we have adhered to a set format. It starts with a Warm-up Game to encourage the group to start working together co-operatively, followed by a 'Round' which enables everybody to make some small contribution to the circle by completing a phrase or 'tag-line'. This is followed by the main Activity. These have been grouped into four sessions which conform to a theme. To get the most out of each activity, we have suggested that each one is then *Conferenced*. This will include thought provoking discussion and a time for reflection about the learning that has taken place. Teachers are able to unravel and give balance to learning situations and ensure the best possible outcome. Opportunities to extend the work can follow on from the conference. The Circle-time ends with a concluding game to round off the session and allow the group to reunite as well as enlivening the proceedings after a heavy discussion period.

The set format is there for teachers to use as they stand or to 'pick and mix' as they wish! The techniques used in Circle-time will be discussed in the next chapter.

Relationships

The ability to communicate effectively with others is a large part of being able to function interpersonally and an important task of childhood learning is to form positive relationships. Children need to understand how friendships are developed and maintained and in order for this to happen they must also acquire the ability to look at things from another person's point of view. Through discussion and role play activities, Circle-time can be used as a practice ground for recognising that other people may have different perspectives. Working on friendships and relationships is beneficial for both pupils and teachers to gain a better insight into one another and to recognise the ways in which they are alike and the ways in which they differ. 'Joining' children across the circle is a key element. In rounds or tag lines, children who have expressed similar views or experiences are joined together. For example, if a child completes the tag-line 'Today I feel.....' with the word 'worried' and someone else expresses the same view, the teacher can say, 'Jody feels like that too.' This reduces a sense of isolation and opens the view that other people have similar feelings.

In order to foster meaningful relationships it is vital for the teacher to consider interactions between themselves and their pupils. If relationships are not positive there is no immediate modelling occurring. A teacher who is seriously concerned with helping pupils achieve positive feelings towards themselves and others needs to answer the following questions :

- 'How can people feel liked unless someone likes them ?'

- 'How can people feel accepted unless someone accepts them ?'

- 'How can people feel they have dignity and integrity unless someone treats them as if they do?'

- 'How can people feel they are able unless somewhere they experience success ?'

(Coombes 1985)

Teachers' attitudes and perceptions are instrumental in forming a child's self-image. In other words the child who thinks well of himself will behave reasonably. The teacher will perceive him favourably. The teacher's favourable perceptions and expectations fuel the pupil's self-regard. The pupil continues to behave appropriately and so the cycle continues. The child who has a history of failure comes to school thinking badly of him or herself and behaves in accordance with this opinion. The teacher is likely to regard the child unfavourably and this is sensed by the pupil who slips further down the spiral, culminating in low self-esteem.

Communication

Good communication is fundamental to building positive relationships. Being able to get in touch with our feelings and emotions and being able to communicate these to others is an important aspect of Circle-time work and the cornerstone to any problem solving or conflict resolution. The ability to express thoughts clearly and to listen to the other person's point of view is an essential element when trying to resolve a dispute. Active listening is a skill that is taught in Circle-time to facilitate this process. Children who can learn to articulate their feelings are seen not to allow fears and worries to build up and can gain release through expression. Once pupils have come to recognise their own emotions they are better placed to understand those of others.

Non-verbal forms of communication are also explored in Circle-time, as studies have shown that words are often the least important part of any message. The way a face looks, the tone of voice used or the posture adopted by a person carries far more impact than words alone. These unspoken elements betray a person's innermost thoughts, feelings and motivations and pupils need to cue into these signs and become skilful at recognising them in themselves and others.

Trust

Circle-time aims to create an atmosphere of mutual trust, where children feel safe and able to try out strategies in a non-blaming environment. Confidentiality is an essential requirement in Circle-time. Initially it is helpful to have an unwritten contract with children that whatever is declared in Circle-time is private and must not be disclosed outside the circle unless permission is given, as in the case when information is shared in pairs. Children need to feel comfortable and confident and able to express themselves without fear of ridicule and it is useful to have a rule that we do not name individuals when talking about anything negative. During Circle-time discussions, there is a rule that children exhibit trust for one another by listening to each other without interrupting and without any comments or 'put-downs'. Building trust is a gradual and continual process.

Occasionally a teacher may hear information that cannot remain secret and must be passed on to the appropriate agency. In that case the teacher should talk to the child in private and follow the LEA's guidelines.

Self-esteem

Research has shown a strong link between a child's self-esteem and academic success. Children who feel good about themselves learn more easily and retain information longer. Many teachers may feel that in today's classroom, with all the pressures of the National Curriculum, there is little time to devote to anything else. However taking the time to raise children's self-esteem will be time well spent as pupils who feel good about themselves will have positive attitudes to work and will be more likely to succeed. The child with high self-esteem is also likely to be confident in social situations and not be afraid when tackling new ideas in school. It's rather like going into the 'penny arcade' with a pocket full of coins. When you have plenty of change you can play the machines and afford to risk losing some, after all there will still be enough left. However, if you continue to lose, you become like the child with low self-esteem. You have little money and cannot afford to gamble as you run the risk of failing and being left with nothing. Persistent failure, or when a child is labelled 'stupid' or 'lazy' enough times, is like the slow drip of the Chinese water torture – if it happens enough times, or if they keep hearing it, children will come to accept it as the truth. Children eventually fulfil the prophecy they think others expect of them. Circle-time is a way of supporting children with low self-esteem by making it a safe environment in which to take risks without the fear of failure.

Both the level of self-esteem and the process through which self-esteem is determined are derived through relationships and interactions with others. The groups to which we belong and the social support they provide have important and powerful effects on one's self-esteem. Interactions with group members provides support, opportunities and models for pro-social behaviour. Self-esteem can be enhanced through the co-operative experiences of Circle-time. The social and personal experiences they gain will be the path to the effective growth of self.

Self-esteem is explored more fully in a later chapter.

Co-operation

Co-operative games and activities help to build and support a caring environment in which to play and learn. Much of the work in a classroom is individual and competitive which can lead to success or failure. Circle-time activities and games are structured to ensure there are no winners or losers and that each child's participation is necessary for the group to succeed. Working with other children is often less stressful and being a valued member of a group can be affirming, encouraging awareness and acceptance. Activities are designed to encourage children to listen to the other person's point of view and find outcomes to allow both parties to achieve their goal. This means that every child is a valuable member of the class and is a valued person in their own right.

Working in groups

Successful teaching involves working in groups. Group work enables children to understand themselves and how they interact with others. The teaching and learning process involved should encourage pupils to be sensitive to the needs of others in order to develop satisfactory relationships. Not all children know instinctively how to interact effectively, nor do interpersonal group skills magically appear when needed. Pupils must be taught these skills and motivated to use them. Working co-operatively and collaboratively in a group is not easy and consequently classes very often settle into a pattern of groups which is simply a collection of individuals, unaware of one another's needs, producing outcomes that are not satisfactory for anyone.

With careful planning and organisation, the class teacher can facilitate effective group work, where group members can offer support and provide opportunities and models for pro-social behaviour. It has been found that enabling groups to function successfully has proved to be extremely effective in supporting children with difficulties and in raising the skill level of everyone.

Conflict resolution

Conflicts are an inevitable part of school life due to its members having different opinions, interests and goals, but conflict need not be an unhealthy situation if we learn and grow from the outcome. Children come to school with varying skills for avoiding conflict and teachers are in a central position to develop and teach their pupils a wide range of strategies enabling them to have a real choice about their behaviour. So many times children repeat the same ineffectual solution to a problem which leads to confrontation or rejection. Circle-time is the ideal forum for discussing conflicts in a non-emotional environment and for discovering alternative solutions and strategies. It gives children the time and space to consider their own or other people's actions that may have contributed to the conflict and allows them to do so in a calm environment. As each class builds up its own repertoire of solutions, individual repertoires widen and start to act as a preventative measure so that fewer conflicts arise in the class and playground. Together a class can work through its problems and work towards forming a cohesive group. The children begin to see how much they have in common with one another instead of seeing their differences. The spirit of competition becomes replaced by an atmosphere of empathy and mutual assistance.

Circle-time and children with special educational needs

Much of the work in Circle-time is active and oral as opposed to the majority of school work where there is a heavy emphasis on reading and writing. This means that children with learning difficulties will not suffer the disadvantage they experience in other areas of the curriculum. They will not stand out as being different in the circle, the pair or the small group. There is support for these pupils not only from the teacher but most importantly from their peers. This work fosters a caring, helping environment, as it is essentially co-operative rather than competitive. Circle-time can bring positive benefits for everyone as they all work together to ensure that there are no losers or failures.

Teachers who are new to Circle-time may be wary of including the child with behaviour problems, but usually difficult pupils work well in this less pressurised type of learning situation. They respond in an environment where they are valued and listened to and where they feel more in control. This does not mean that there are never any discipline problems in this type of work – there can be, and the teacher still needs to be a facilitator who can bring order back to the proceedings. The difference is that the teacher is not solely responsible for what happens to the group. The group can look to its own behaviour in relation to the rules and agreements reached by all parties. The skill of the teacher is needed here in order to create a group atmosphere in which all pupils become willing and able to learn as one cohesive and co-operative group. Getting feedback from other people about how we are perceived is a highly educational experience, and the group can help an individual to recognise positive aspects about themselves. Raising self-esteem and helping pupils feel good about themselves means that there is less need for showing off and attention seeking. Children with behaviour problems often feel excluded but will feel discouraged from misbehaving if they feel they are beginning to belong to a group. The group will want to help the child as there will be less discord in class, providing a better working atmosphere, and they will enjoy the opportunity to contribute to improving the situation. Behaviour is a set of skills and can be taught and learnt. These skills will empower pupils to be able to take increasing control and responsibility for their behaviour.

As well as children with learning difficulties and behaviour problems, there are also children with emotional difficulties. Children who are withdrawn, even isolated from their peer group, pupils who are quiet or silent in discussion and keep themselves 'out of reach' of the teacher. Circle-time activities enable these pupils to be included and a sense of belonging and confidence begins to develop. Initially, these children should be encouraged to talk with just one other person and for any discussion to be private. This encourages the shy child to participate as he or she is only having to face an audience of one. The same can be said for children with speech difficulties. They must feel safe and comfortable before being invited to speak. The teacher must set the ground rules to ensure that ridicule and hostility is not permitted. Once they feel confident with speaking group numbers can increase to sharing with three or four before working up to the whole group. In whole class discussions, the opportunity to 'pass' must always be there so as not to make this a threatening time, but one that can be enjoyed and where children can see that there are no right or wrong answers and that whatever is said is OK.

CHAPTER 2 – TECHNIQUES

Seating Arrangements

It is important to create a relaxed, comfortable atmosphere for Circle-time and it is therefore best to start by letting the children sit where they like. This will usually mean sitting next to a friend or boys sitting next to boys and there are times when this is quite acceptable. However, there are also times when friends do not work well together, when certain pairings will lead to confrontations and when certain children can become isolated. Rather than being prescriptive, teachers can use games to get the group moving and mix up the class. This way the children will not realise they are being moved as they will be too busy having fun! Most of the warm-up games used in Chapter 4 are designed for this purpose. This enables children to mix with those they might normally have little to do with and allows the opportunity for exploring new friendships and the possibilities that there are other people with whom they have something in common – 'I didn't know you liked motorbikes too'.

Any children sitting together need to be reminded that they are responsible for their own behaviour and that if they behave inappropriately there will be consequences. Consequences need to be 'spelled out' to children so that they can make a choice as to whether the consequence will occur.

For example:

Teacher: 'Sam I want you to keep your hands to yourself. You are stopping Ben from listening and if you continue you will have to leave the circle. The choice is yours.'

If the child continues to misbehave then the consequence is imposed with the words, 'You have chosen to leave the circle.' When the child feels that he or she is ready, then he or she can be invited to rejoin the circle.

Gaining Quiet

An agreed signal to which everyone adheres ensures that schedules are kept and that no one person is given extra attention. This needs to be achieved in a quiet calm manner as shouting above the noise is stressful for the teacher, creates tension and is not a good role model for pupils.

Signals can be :

- an arm raised. When the teacher raises his or her arm, it is a signal to pupils to conclude their conversation. They, in turn, signal the completion by all of them raising an arm until the whole group is sitting in silence with their arms raised. This usually only takes a few minutes, so no need for aching arms!

- 'arms folded' can indicate it is time for pairs or groups to stop talking, or children can be encouraged to fold arms when they have finished sharing thoughts.

- write, 'QUIET' on a piece of card. Hold it up at the appropriate moment. When the whole group has complied, turn the card round to show the other side on which is written: 'THANK YOU'.

When children are not adhering to the signal then play the *waiting game.*

Try not to enter into unnecessary confrontations in which the child is forced on to the defensive and a win-lose situation develops. Just sit quietly in a relaxed pose doing nothing. Other pupils will see that you are waiting and will join in putting peer pressure on others to conform. This exercise requires patience on the part of the teacher but is important as it encourages children to be responsible for their own behaviour.

Children really enjoy playing the games and extra games can be used as a reward for appropriate behaviour.

Active Listening

An important aspect of any Circle-time activity is the skill of *active listening*. This is a skill that both children and adults need to practise - we often think we are listening, but giving our full attention when someone is speaking is a skill we need to cultivate.

Active listening can be defined as:

1. having eye contact with the person who is talking;

2. giving full attention;

3. sitting quietly without distracting the person who is speaking;

4. focusing on the speaker's needs;

5. showing that you understand;

6. letting the speaker express feelings without interruptions or 'put-downs';

7. asking no questions;

8. making no comments of your own;

9. show you are listening by smiling, nodding etc. at appropriate times;

10. communicating acceptance – that no matter what is said the speaker is still OK.

The Chinese have a very apt character for the verb 'to listen' which sums it up succinctly:

EAR

YOU

EYES

UNDIVIDED ATTENTION

HEART

Active listening is important to provide an atmosphere of co-operation and mutual regard. This is also beneficial to the teacher as they no longer need to be agreeing, disagreeing, arguing, praising or blaming and can therefore take a neutral role which enables others in the group to express their feelings. Listening skills represent a necessary step in the effective functioning of Circle-time.

The 'Round'

Discussion time usually takes the form of a **round**. The round is an opportunity for each person in the circle to make a statement or a contribution to whatever the group is discussing. One person starts, sometimes with an opening tag-line and the turn moves round the circle until everyone who wants to has had the opportunity to contribute. No one may comment on what anyone else has said and this includes the teacher.

One person speaking at a time, and everyone else listening, is an important Circle-time rule. It gives everyone an equal chance to contribute without being shouted down or ridiculed. It also encourages the quieter children to participate and denies the more vocal elements of the class the chance to dominate.

To facilitate the rule of only one person talking at a time, especially with younger children, it is sometimes useful to have a tangible object to pass round indicating who's turn it is to speak and this is often known as **the magic microphone**. An alternative to this is a **talk ticket** which is a piece of card that again is a visible signal to remind everyone that only the person with the ticket can talk.

The aim of a round is to provide a structure to get children to communicate with one another. All ideas are valued equally. The opportunity to **'pass'** is there for each individual as this is not to be a threatening time where pupils believe they are going to be forced to do something against their will. This would be totally counter productive to the aims of Circle-time. Initially no comment should be made about pupils who pass because if rounds are introduced in a very non-threatening way then children can begin to enjoy the experience and see that there are no right or wrong answers and that whatever is said is OK. If pupils pass just say something like: 'Its all right! I expect you need some thinking time. We'll come back to you.' At the end of the round ask again. Very often, a response is then offered as ideas are shared and thoughts triggered.

For young children rounds can start off with simple tag-lines such as:

'My favourite colour is ... '

'My best friend is ... '

'My favourite TV. programme is ... '

'I feel happy when ... '

'I feel sad when ... '

Later, as the pupils become accustomed to this way of working, they can choose topics to discuss which arise from incidents in school or in the playground, and then use them as a forum for brainstorming ideas and strategies as a means of resolving conflicts.

This gives the chance to explore self-awareness in a positive way before leading on to more sensitive areas. It takes time to build trust where one feels comfortable exploring personal feelings with other group members. It also takes a while for children to recognise the importance of establishing trust, for them to trust another person to have a valid comment and for them to exhibit that trust by respecting their words without interruption or comment.

Problems can occur with this technique when children are first starting or when there are large numbers in a class. It may be unreasonable to ask children to sit for a long period of time without an activity other than 'active listening' as they can become distracted which in turn could lead to them disturbing others. If these problems are occurring, use the whole class round less frequently. Instead ask children to share ideas in pairs, threes or fours. This way everybody is occupied and it also encourages shy children to participate as they are only having to face an audience of one. Feedback can be given by appointing a spokesperson from each group.

A variation on the round is **double circles**. The inner circle faces outwards and the outer circle faces in. Each person sits opposite a partner. A subject or tag-line is given for discussion and taking it in turns each pupil talks and then listens. Initially pupils may need to be labelled A and B so that first of all the A's talk and the B's listen, and then they swap. After an appropriate time, a signal is given and the inner circle move one space to the right. The same subject can be used or a new development introduced. Each time the circle moves everyone has a new partner and can hear new ideas or rehearse thoughts and opinions.

It is then possible to return to a large circle to report back to the group on your partner's interests or thoughts on a subject, providing you have their permission. This introduces another element as concentration and good listening skills are necessary for effective and accurate reporting to take place.

This book contains 40 tag-lines that could be used in a round. Here are some more suggestions:

Feelings

I feel important when ...

I feel proud when ...

When I can't do my work I feel ...

When I am in school I feel ...

Affirmation

My favourite food is ...

My favourite place is ...

I am good at ...

I can ...

Caring

The world would be a better place if people would ...

If I had three wishes they would be ...

The thing I care most about is ...

I can show that I care for others by ...

Friendship

My friends like me because ...

My friends could help me by ...

My friends like it when I ...

My friends don't like it when I ...

Co-operation

When I need help I wish others would ...

When we work together we need to ...

I could help others by ...

Working in a group is good because ...

Gender

I think boys should ...

I think girls should ...

Boys can help girls to be ...

Girls can help boys to be ...

Changes

If I could change my name it would be ...

If I could change where I live I would live ...

I wish I could change ...

When I first came to this class I remember ...

Conflict Resolution

I am sorry that ...

I get into trouble when I ...

I get angry when ...

The thing that makes me really mad is ...

Problem Solving

If I had a hundred pounds I would buy ...

If I were a grown up I would ...

If I could change one thing about this classroom it would be ...

If I could do what I like I would ...

Reception

I am happy when ...

I am sad when ...

My favourite colour is ...

My favourite TV programme is ...

The Activity

The activity is the central part of any Circle-time around which the other components hinge. It is therefore essential that this section is well prepared so that children are not kept waiting whilst the teacher organises resources. Inappropriate behaviour can very quickly develop if children have nothing to do or if they think the teacher's attention is engaged elsewhere.

Teachers need to be aware that the pairings or grouping of children may need to be managed in order to ensure that children are given the opportunity to work with many different people and to feel comfortable about doing so. Care needs to also be taken to make sure that certain children do not become isolated or continually rejected.

The activities in the book have been linked together in sets of four to form themes. This is useful as teachers are then able to extend the work into other areas of the curriculum. There is also a logical progression in the work which allows for reflection and the opportunity to explore subjects in greater depth.

An Example of an Activity: Caring Hands Tree (see page 65)

The children are all sitting round in a circle and I get out a large sheet of paper and put it on the floor in the middle of the circle.

'Who wants to join the green hand gang?' I ask, smiling. I say this because I know from previous experience that when I draw round the children's hands I will get green felt tip pen on them. Never mind, it's water proof, and anyway children don't seem to mind getting dirty! A sea of hands goes up and I select about ten children and proceed to draw round their hands making sure they are all at the top of the page with fingers pointing upwards. The children sit quietly in anticipation, waiting to see what I am going to do with these green hands.

I take the brown felt tip pen and begin to join the hands together with thin lines, gradually widening to form a trunk. Smiles pass round the circle as the penny drops. 'What do you think I'm going to do with it now I've drawn the tree?' The children put up their hands as they know I do not accept answers from those who call out. Our warm-up game was all to do with things you can do with your hands and very soon someone suggests that this is what we might be doing. I write the words, 'Caring Hands Tree', at the bottom of the sheet and ask the children to think of one kind, caring thing they could do with their hands. We take the magic microphone (someone in the class has made one from a table tennis ball stuck on the end of a toilet roll cardboard tube) and pass it round the circle so that everyone gets a chance to talk and to be listened to I continue to sit on the floor in the middle and write each suggestion on a hand, or in a space nearby.

The children have now been sitting for a little while and it's time to change the format of the activity to give variety and to encourage greater participation. I divide the class into four groups and appoint a group leader for each one. The four groups make four separate circles and the leader is given a large sheet of paper with a green and brown felt tip pen. They are then told to repeat the exercise and draw round each person's hand and form a tree. We have done groupwork before and the children know the rules about taking turns. Only one person speaking at a time and making sure everyone is included. This time each group is instructed to think of hurtful things that hands can do. I wander round to give help if needed and listen to the comments.

'I hate it when the boys pull my hair - it's a real cold prickly.'

'I hate it when someone makes a rude gesture to you. It makes you hurt inside just as much as if they had hit you.'

'Why is it that hands can be so clever and yet so horrible?'

I give each group the signal that we will finish in two minutes and then we all sit back in the large circle to share our findings with one another and conference the results.

The Conference

The conference section of the Circle-time is a crucial element. It follows each activity and allows for discussion and evaluation of the subject. It is a time to encourage children to offer their ideas, thoughts, feelings and for the teacher to also have an input in order to steer the discussion in certain directions if necessary, so that children understand the point of the exercise. The conferencing needs to be carefully thought out in order to stimulate appropriate responses with questions such as :

How will that work?

How will that affect other people?

How do people feel about that?

Children also need to be reminded of the confidentiality rule - that we do not name individuals when talking about anything negative. Children can say something like, 'I had a Cold Prickly yesterday when someone called me a name.'

The conference section will also allow teachers to evaluate the success of each Circle-time as they receive feedback from the group which will help in any future planning.

An Example of a Conference: Caring Hands Tree (see page 65)

The children re-convene in a large circle after finishing the activity. Each group spreads its large sheet in the middle of the circle for all to see. Later these will transfer to our Circle-time notice board and remain there for the week to remind children of the current topic.

I ask the children to look at the sheets and say, 'What does it feel like when people do something kind or caring for you with their hands?, and, 'What does it feel like when people hurt you with their hands?' The children pass the magic microphone round and I write down their comments on a large sheet of paper divided into two columns.

'One of the things I hate about the playground is being hit and pushed around. It makes me feel empty inside'.

Another child makes a similar statement and I am able to join these two -   ' Sophie feels like that too'.

This allows children to see they are not alone in their feelings and enables me to store the information for a future Circle-time. Being able to identify and recognise feelings is an essential ingredient to a successful Circle-time. It will empower children and enable them to cope with confrontations in a non-aggressive manner. For example, a member of the circle says, 'I feel unhappy when people put two fingers up to me,' which allows me the opportunity to teach children to use the 'I statement' and say, ' I like you, but I don't like it when you gesture at me.' Several of the children want to practise this and we have an impromptu drama session in pairs with each child playing both parts. '

I never knew what to do before and used to get cross and hit people because they had hurt me. Now I shall try this. I can't promise to do it every time but I will try.'

We end by looking at both trees and deciding that this week we will really try to have caring hands and not hurtful hands.

During the week there are still one or two instances of unkind use of hands but I am able to say, 'Was that a caring hand or a hurtful hand?' We are able to have a starting point for a dialogue and children can make it right by choosing something from the Caring Hands Tree to do to make amends. I also hear other children using this as a tool for self-correction and take heart that the slow drip drip is getting the message over!

Brainstorming

One effective technique for gathering ideas about a specific issue or problem is brainstorming.

The four main purposes of brainstorming are:

- to produce a large number of ideas quickly;
- to encourage pupils to think creatively and look for original ideas;
- to involve the whole class and show that we value everybody's ideas;
- to show that by working co-operatively we can achieve more than the individual can alone.

Ideas can be written down on a central piece of paper and the teacher can act as a scribe for younger children. The atmosphere should be non-judgemental with everybody's ideas being valued and written down (no matter how impractical) without being commented on. The teacher, who is also part of the group, can add ideas, scattering them in a random order so as not to perceive one as being better than another.

When the flow of ideas ceases it is a good idea to wait for a few minutes so that children can understand that they are responsible for their own learning and that the teacher is not there dictating terms. Silence gives an opportunity for reflective thinking and it takes the teacher away from rescue mode. It seems second nature for teachers to leap in and rescue the situation whenever there is an awkward silence. This handing over of responsibility of learning to our pupils is something that we as teachers need to cultivate.

After the pupils have exhausted their suggestions the list should be reviewed. Categorise and simplify if appropriate or list the ideas in some order of importance. The group is then in a better position to make choices and decisions.

This is a useful tool when discussing behaviour as pupils are stimulated into donating ideas to solve problems which can lead to the formation of a bank of solutions for pupils to try in similar circumstances. This will ultimately help to provide positive role models for unskilled children and arm them with a list of strategies to attempt.

The fact that all contributions are accepted and anonymous, that no one is excluded or evaluated, that most of the time they are not under the watchful eye of the teacher (busy acting as a scribe) all add up to a positive feeling within the group.

Each person is valued and valuable, equal with everyone else and has the feeling that their contributions are necessary and will be heard.

Rules

Circle-time is flexible but, as with all successful structures, there needs to be some consensus of what is acceptable behaviour. Rules are important as they provide a framework within which relationships can develop and grow in a positive way. As with general classroom rules, it is best to have as few as possible, but to constantly reinforce and reward adherence. They need to be written up and displayed in the classroom and they need to be flexible to accommodate the changing needs of the group.

With young children three rules are sufficient and these could be:

1. Only one person speaks at a time.

2. We listen to the person who is speaking.

3. Have fun and make sure you don't spoil anybody else's fun!

Older children will be able to discuss the whole area of rules, perhaps starting with the rules they experience when playing games, what they thought their function was or if they thought they were fair. Pupils can brainstorm ideas for Circle-time rules, negotiate priorities with their peers and then select the ones they wish to operate. This way they will own the rules and therefore be much more likely to adhere to them. They constitute a contract between group members and eventually those members will begin to take responsibility for reminding one another when they transgress. This takes the pressure from the teacher being the law enforcing authority, as children learn from one another, rather than being dictated to. Some rules which groups have evolved are:

• Listen to one another.

• Talk one at a time.

• Respect the ideas and values of others.

• Take responsibility for your own behaviour.

• The right to pass is always there.

• It's OK to make mistakes, as they are valuable learning points.

• Keep agreements that are made with the group.

• Do not hurt anybody, either physically or verbally.

Games

The structure of Circle-time will vary with the age of the children, their experiences of working together as a group and other similar variables. Games can be used as a warm up activity for the group to get into the spirit of co-operation, of working and playing together for fun. They can be used for concluding a session as a way of reuniting the group before going off to separate classroom activities and for enlivening the proceedings after a heavy discussion period. Games also allow for legitimate movement and are a good way to split inappropriate pairings or the gender split where the girls sit on one side of the circle and the boys on the other!

Games are included in Circle-time as they are not only fun activities with much affirming taking place when individuals are named or chosen, but they are also useful as starting points for further discussions e.g. Was there anyone not chosen?

'How did it feel? Could we as a group have done anything to avoid it happening?' These discussions could then be widened to encompass other areas of conflict such as the playground. The group could discuss how it might feel for children who do not have anyone to play with, or who do not get chosen for games, and the types of strategies that children could employ to create a more harmonious atmosphere whereby they are not being selfish but are thinking of others. Very often, this will lead children to establish rules to make sure everyone is included and to incorporate the notion of fair play.

Circle-time games are co-operative not competitive and winning is not an important factor.

Games are useful as they can:

1.   provide a structure for learning.

2.   defuse tension;

3.   initiate group work skills;

4.   build trust and sensitivity;

5.   provide an opportunity for everyone to participate;

6.   break down pupil / teacher barriers;

7.   promote good communication;

8.   improve group functioning;

9.   increase self-awareness;

10. increase concentration and time on-task;

11. improve listening skills;

12. encourage creativity and lateral thinking

13. enhance academic achievement;

14. enhance self-esteem.

Games can be used as 'energy raisers'. After a game, great energy and enthusiasm can be put into work which follows, making games a great investment in time.

An important feature not to be ignored is Circle-time's potential for engendering fun and laughter. This is a primary motivational factor which ensures that pupils are always cued in to the 'here and now' and remain alert. If humour can be shared with pupils as a result of teachers participating as an equal member of the group, then it can function to strengthen relationships and create a more trusting climate.

Journals and Think Books

Some children find it too threatening to actually voice their thoughts and feelings and yet, like others, they need an outlet for their emotions. Making a journal or think book is a helpful option as it provides an alternative means for children to express feelings, thoughts or anxieties. They can write down some of those concerns that are worrying them and by committing them to paper feel a release of tension that could otherwise burden the child. Some pupils would find it helpful for the teacher to respond to their concerns by writing back in the journal, or just acknowledging in some way that they understand the problem and that it is OK. Other children might wish for their thoughts to remain their own, and this privacy should be respected. Journals can contain parts that are private as well as parts to share. This dialogue between teachers and pupils will serve to enhance relationships which will have positive outcomes in the classroom.

The teacher can use the journal as an opportunity for pupils to write their thoughts and feelings as if in a diary or they can write tag lines, similar to those used in the 'round', in the book to be used as starters. Examples of items the journal may contain are :

All about me – my family, my friends, my hobbies, things I like to do, my favourite food, etc.

My feelings
- I feel excited when ...
- I feel disappointed when ...
- I feel afraid when ...
- I feel nervous when ...
- I feel angry when ...

have concrete examples of each

My thoughts
- I think I am good at ...
- I think I would like to ...
- I think I am going to try to ...
- I think I am a good friend because ...
- I think people like me because ...

My concerns
- When I break up with a friend
- When I get teased
- When the teacher tells me off
- When I get my sums wrong

Drawings
- Draw how you see yourself when you are strong
- Draw a picture of something that makes you sad
- Draw a picture of something that makes you happy

Journals and 'think books' help children who are limited in their experiences and those unable to express their thoughts and feelings sufficiently due to lack of a wide personal vocabulary.

Using Stories

Another technique in Circle-time is to use stories to illustrate the issue under discussion. This enables the topic to be looked at safely through the eyes of the characters in the stories. Stories can also be used to examine behaviours and feelings from different perspectives, enabling children to see different points of view.

Examples:

The Teddy Robber by Ian Beck (Picture Corgi) – losing a treasured possession.

Not a Worry in the World by Marcia Williams (Walker) – how to cope with worries.

Borka by John Burningham (Red Fox) – teasing.

It Was Jake! by Anita Jeram (Walker) – telling 'tales'.

Tall Inside by J. Richardson (Picture Puffins) – teasing.

The Practical Princess by Jay Williams (Hippo Books) – 'modern fairy stories' from a girl's viewpoint.

Mr. Gumpy's Outing by John Burningham (Picture Puffin) – co-operation and working together.

'The Maligned Wolf' by Leif Fearn in *Global Teacher, Global Learner* (Hodder and Stoughton) – Red Riding Hood seen through the wolf's eyes.

Stories can be used as a starting point and for opening up a discussion.

Recording Information

Circle-time book

As Circle-time work becomes a regular feature in your class or school, it is useful to write down information, strategies, thoughts and feelings and make a list of ideas. These can then act as a point of reference, a bank of possible solutions and a record of what has been discussed. On-going concerns can be registered for future discussion. Pupils can be encouraged to contribute ideas and individuals can take it in turn to record agreed data.

Feelings board

This could be a board or a large piece of card displaying all the feelings words verbalised or identified during Circle-time sessions. It will help build and extend the emotional vocabulary of the pupils. By being able to precisely verbalise feelings children are less likely to 'bottle up' thoughts and feelings which will lessen the likelihood of aggressive outbursts or sudden bursts of temper. Being able to say how you feel and to voice an opinion in a positive way is a skill that can be taught and practised in Circle-time to enable children to be able to utilise these skills at other times when the need arises.

Celebration book

We all need a regular 'pat on the back' and what better way to record successes than to write them in a celebration book. The book can be left in the classroom and the staffroom where children and adults can be encouraged to write about the positive behaviours of pupils (and staff). These can then be shared once a week at a celebration assembly where the whole school can share in the good things going on in their community. Think of the boost to self-esteem when a child's name is mentioned (for something positive) in assembly. Too often in school the focus is on the negative. Teachers need to be aware and actively reward appropriate behaviour – what gets attention will increase. Look around and 'catch them being good.'

CHAPTER 3 – SELF-ESTEEM

Everyone needs self esteem. When people experience it, they feel good, look good, and are both effective and productive. They respond to others and themselves in healthy, positive, growing ways.

'People who have positive self-esteem know that they are lovable and capable and they care about themselves and other people. They do not have to build themselves up by tearing other people down or by patronising less competent people.' (Illsley-Clark 1978.)

In any discussion about self-esteem there are likely to be several definitions. Usually the terms self-concept, ideal self and self-image will appear somewhere. **Self-concept** is composed of all the beliefs and attitudes one holds about oneself, and is the umbrella term under which the other three aspects develop.

'The self concept is the individual's awareness of his/her own self. It is an awareness of one's identity.' (Lawrence, 1987.)

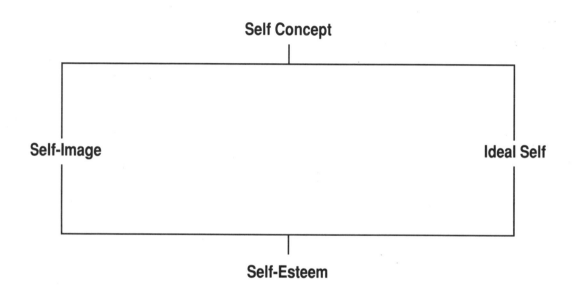

Self Concept

Self-Image

Ideal Self

Self-Esteem

Self-image is the picture that we have of ourselves, both academically and physically. From our earliest moments of life, we begin to accumulate information about ourselves and the world in which we live. We receive messages from those around us about being loved, clever, lazy and so forth. These signals can be non-verbal as well as verbal. By the time children reach school age, they are beginning to form their self concept and their reactions to learning and to school. The social and emotional climate of the classroom will be determined by the beliefs and attitudes which they have of themselves.

The process of development of the self-image has been referred to as the 'looking-glass theory of self' (Cooley, 1902) because each child is forming his or her self-image as he or she receives feedback from others. The role of feedback would seem to have a significant importance in the classroom situation where children are constantly being evaluated and judged. The child who thinks well of himself will get on with his or her work and will behave appropriately. The teacher will perceive that child favourably. The teacher's favourable perceptions and expectations fuel the pupil's self-regard, and so the cycle continues. If a child comes to school thinking badly of him or herself he or she will probably behave in accordance with this opinion. The teacher is likely to regard that child unfavourably. This will be sensed by the child who slips further down the ladder, culminating in low self-esteem. He or she may withdraw, not bother trying, or try to maintain some status by taking on the role of the 'class clown'. A child's poor self-image may also lead him or her to feel ashamed or guilty and become anxious about school work. It is therefore important to realise how vital teacher's perceptions and expectations are in forming a positive self-image that can lead to high self-esteem.

Positive Reinforcement Triangle

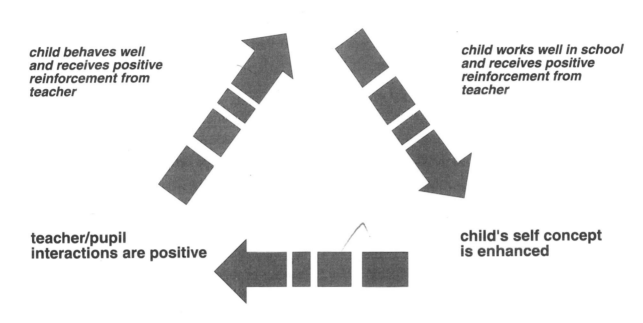

Negative Reinforcement Triangle

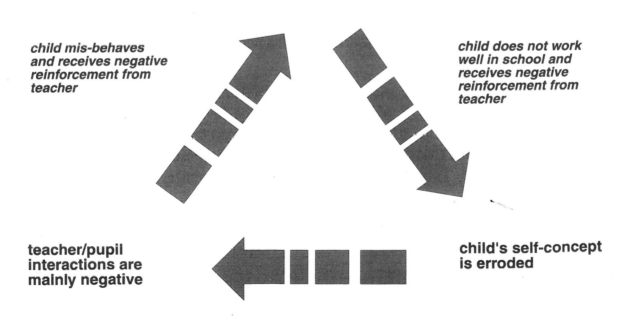

Ideal self is the picture of ourselves as we would like to be. Alongside the development of self-image children are learning that there are ideal characteristics they should possess and that there are ideal standards of behaviour that are valued by society.

Self-esteem is a personal evaluation of the difference between the self-image and the ideal self. If the difference is too great, then low self-esteem occurs and children can become despondent about themselves and develop a poor self-image in relation to others.

All children experience a low self-esteem at times as it is a normal reaction when they fall below the expectations they have of themselves, or of others who are important to them. A low self-esteem is not a problem in itself, providing that children have a reservoir of good feelings about themselves and providing that those around them act in an appropriate manner so as to enable children to learn by their mistakes. It is not always failure that leads to a low self-esteem, rather it is often the way significant people in their lives – parents, peers, and especially teachers – react to that failure. Teachers are in a very strong position to be able to influence self-esteem.

Listen in the classroom for the child who is constantly saying, 'I can't do that', and not having a go. Children like this even set themselves up for failure because when they fail, it's the one time they have been successful. – 'There you are! I told you I couldn't do it.' Children with low self-esteem will often destroy work – even when it is good, refusing to believe that their image has altered.

When teachers are wanting to change this belief they need to be aware of the child's sensitivities and start by praising privately until they feel the child is ready to receive public praise. They should show that they value the child and his or her work and rescue it before it is scribbled on, or destroyed. If the child continues to fail in areas which are valued by the significant people in his or her life, then overall self-esteem will be affected. The behaviour of teachers and the attitudes which they hold towards pupils is a vital ingredient in fostering a positive self-regard.

Common characteristics of children with low self esteem:

1. They are often isolated. Their own feeling of poor self-worth may lead them to believe that others view them in the same light. They are reluctant to take the risk of making overtures in case they are rejected.

2. They can have feelings of inadequacy and worthlessness and see themselves as inferior. They are lacking in confidence, and are unsure of themselves. Other children may cover up this feeling of inadequacy by acting the clown and 'showing off,' seeming at first glance to be full of confidence. In fact, the opposite is true. The display is a coping strategy, to gain some status within the peer group, even if it is only that of the class joker.

3. They under-achieve in school. They also tend to avoid work, and use a number of delaying tactics. In classroom tasks they avoid the risk of failure by delaying getting started for as long as possible. For example, teachers may need to take the risks for children e.g. 'I know this is difficult, but I think you can do it, have a try!'. Or, when the child gets things wrong use the right kind of encouragement, for example 'Don't worry! This is my fault. I obviously didn't explain very well. Let me try again.'

4. Children with low esteem can be anxious, seeking for approval and needing a lot of reassurance from their teachers and peers.

5. They set unrealistic goals for themselves which are either too high or too low. For example if you stand

children in front of a waste bin and ask them to toss a beanbag into the bin from a distance (the children being allowed to choose the distance) you can often tell the child with low self-esteem as they will be the one attempting to toss the bean bag from one end of the room to the other. Needless to say the child usually fails – but then, he or she is setting his or herself up to fail as in this way, no risks are involved. The child knows the outcome from the start. These children already have a low opinion of themselves and this failure just seeks to confirm this view.

6. Children with low self-regard tend to be more disruptive. This may be to do with their feelings of frustration and anger at their sense of failure. Disruption is also a way of getting teachers' attention. Children learn from a very young age that, while they are quiet and getting on, there is little adult interaction. Children realise that if they are successful and get all the answers right, then they get teacher's approval and attention. Children with low self-esteem who are under-achieving are not receiving the attention they need through work, so they look for other means for getting attention. They quickly find that being disruptive gets teacher's attention immediately! This often has negative consequences but is preferable to no recognition at all. Teachers need to be aware of these problems and should teach children the necessary skills to enable them to receive positive attention. Teachers need then, to look around the classroom frequently and 'catch them being good'. Children will the make the connection between appropriate behaviour and teacher attention. To make this easier for children it is useful to remember to be specific when praising, for example, 'Well done Ben! You have remembered to put your hand up before answering.'

7. They are reluctant to join in. Joining in could mean that their failure goes on public display and that could lead to humiliation or ridicule – better not to risk it.

8. Children with low self-esteem rarely seem satisfied with their efforts and sometimes destroy pieces of good work. This is to do with their sense of being 'no good' and any improvement not fitting with their perceived view of themselves. Quite often, they feel the 'failure label' is so firmly hung round their neck that they find it difficult to receive a different message. When children are feeling like this they find it hard to accept public praise, especially when the teacher, excited with any change in behaviour, goes 'over the top.'

9. Children with low self-esteem do not like themselves and therefore believe that nobody else will like them. They may be desperate to make friends but often do not possess the skills to make and maintain friendships. Through affirmation exercises we can prove to children that they are worthwhile individuals and that they are valuable and valued.

10. They do not like being continually criticised (who does!). Talking to children in a manner that informs them of inappropriate behaviour whilst keeping their self-esteem intact is an important skill that adults need to cultivate.

Circle-time is the ideal forum for enhancing self-esteem, as it provides opportunities to encourage individuals and to work in group situations on relationships and social skills. The groups we belong to and the social support which they provide have important and powerful effects on self-esteem. Co-operation and interaction with others promotes the worth of the individual and provides opportunities for promoting pro-social behaviour. The teacher and the class can learn to appreciate one another, both the things they have in common and the things that are different, and learn to work together and play together in a harmonious atmosphere.

Talking to Children

How many times have you heard these statements in a classroom, or ones that are similar?

'You silly boy!' 'You baby. Children in the reception class behave better than that.'

'You clumsy child.' 'You are such a lazy child.'

In Circle-time, you may wish speak to a child about his or her inappropriate behaviour. However it is very easy to be negative at these times. These negative statements are referred to as 'YOU Statements.' They imply that the pupil is the problem. The child with low self-esteem will accept this as confirmation of his or her own opinion of him or herself. The impact of the message relies on the authority of the adult and is therefore open to confrontation with one winner and one loser. Notice too, how easy it is to shout when delivering a 'You' statement as you stand there wagging your finger and towering over the child!

An alternative is an 'I Statement.' This is where the adult communicates his or her feelings and gives children information about their behaviour and its effect. This is not an attack on the person but on their behaviour and therefore protects the self-concept and reduces the likelihood of confrontation.

> **Key point to remember : LABEL THE ACT NOT THE CHILD.**

I Statements have three components:

1. **The behaviour** e.g. pushing someone over.

2. **The effect** e.g. they hurt themselves.

3. **The feelings** e.g. they feel upset.

A good way to start an 'I Statement' is to begin with:

'When you ... ' (label the behaviour);

'... it ...' (give information about the effect);

'and I/he/she feels ... ' (name the feelings).

For example: 'When you interrupt by talking during Circle-time it disturbs people around you. They find it hard to listen and that makes *me* feel irritable.'

'I Statements' do not readily trip off the tongue and may seem a bit cumbersome at first, but persevere, as they are effective and, as with all things, practice makes perfect.

Special Person

During Circle-time one of the children's favourite times is choosing a special person for the day. This is an opportunity for the group to affirm an individual by asking everyone in the circle to say something positive about the pupil. The person chosen usually waits outside the room to heighten anticipation and keep the surprise total. Young children are invited to go outside with a friend and share a book. While the chosen child is outside each person affirms the special person and the affirmations are recorded in some way so that they will be a tangible memento for the pupil to keep.

Older children can record their own statements on a piece of paper which can be collected to form a booklet or the teacher can scribe the comments on a large sheet of paper in the centre of the circle. This is usually done in the form of a 'round' to enable pupils to listen to one another's comments and even if the comments at first seem a little superficial, practice and good role-modelling from the teacher and peers will encourage pupils to look beneath the surface and discover the positive attributes in every child. It is helpful to start the process by using the most popular children as the class will have no difficulty in finding positive attributes. Once the class becomes skilled and sensitive, other children can be included until everybody has had a turn. Other ideas are special person certificates or posters. Finding the meaning of a child's name can add a fresh dimension and enhance their reputation. (Examples can be seen overleaf)

When the list is complete, the special person is invited back into the centre of the circle or by the teacher's side, and the list is read out to them. To witness the response of children who take part in this special day and see them 'beam from ear to ear' as their list is read is almost justification alone for continuing Circle-time. This gives a tremendous boost to self-esteem.

A special person may be awarded a certificate or given a special badge denoting the event. They may be allowed to pick a name for themselves for the day or be allowed some special privileges such as choosing a game, being first in the line, having extra time on the computer etc. The children enjoy these privileges and the rest of class see them as being 'fair'; everybody will get a turn at being special and the nice thing is that they are rewards for just being themselves.

Examples of Special Person

Someone is chosen as 'special person' and they go outside the classroom. They may take a book to look at and a friend to accompany them. Using the 'magic microphone,' with the teacher acting as scribe, the children list the positive attributes that make the pupil special. Here is an example:

Abigaile is special because ...

she is kind;

she is generous;

she writes neatly;

she is a good tennis player;

she helps me with my work;

she likes animals;

she cares when you have no one to play with;

she comforts you when you hurt yourself;

she draws very funny cartoons;

she shares her crayons;

I like her, she's my best friend.

Special Person Car Wash

This version of special person is called 'car wash.' Children line up in twos facing a partner with a small gap in between. The special person stands at the head of the line and walks, with eyes closed, slowly down between the pairs. As they pass, each pupil touches the special person and whispers an affirmation or personal message. All of this 'washes' over the pupil and they emerge glowing from the experience!

Special Person Song

This can be sung to the person who is special for the day, for example:

This is Mollie,

Celebrate,

Sing it with a cheerful heart.

This is Mollie,

Celebrate,

Sing it with a cheerful heart.

SPECIAL PERSON BADGES

Mollie Curry and Carolyn Bromfield, 1994
NASEN Enterprises Ltd.

THIS PAGE MAY BE PHOTOCOPIED

SPECIAL PERSON BOOKLET

Book cover:

My
Special
Book

Inside page:

_____ *is special because ...*

Mollie Curry and Carolyn Bromfield, 1994
NASEN Enterprises Ltd.

The special person today is

Their name means

They are special because

Mollie Curry and Carolyn Bromfield, 1994
NASEN Enterprises Ltd.

All About Me Poster

Name :   **Date :**

Mollie Curry and Carolyn Bromfield, 1994
NASEN Enterprises Ltd.

CHAPTER 4 – GAMES

This chapter is a compilation of all the games in the book. They have been categorised into different types of games serving different functions and are described here for easy reference with page numbers linking back to the themes. The games can be used with all ages but may need to be adapted to suit the ability of your pupils.

Games within the themes are interchangeable and it maybe that you want to choose a different game from this selection or wish to play one of the children's favourites. We have chosen different games for every activity to allow us to introduce as many games as possible.

Helpful Hints

1. Plan which games you want to use so that children do not get bored as this leads to disruptive behaviour.

2. Do not give long, complicated instructions. Demonstrations can be effective, but actually playing a game is the best way of learning.

3. If a game is not working, don't be afraid to stop. Start again with a different one.

4. Tune in to the mood of your class. If they have just had a 'wet playtime' they may need a boisterous game to help them 'let off steam'. If they have had a heavy discussion they might need a lighthearted game.

5. If one or two children are being 'silly,' try some planned ignoring. If their inappropriate behaviour is not being given attention they will probably stop. If they do not, remind them of your Circle-time rules, one of which will be that you cannot spoil anyone else's fun. Ask them to leave the circle and watch until they are ready to rejoin.

6. Explain the purpose of the games to your class and see if it matches their experiences and feelings.

7. Some games work better on chairs and some on the floor. Think about the arrangement of furniture before you begin.

8. Make sure everyone in the room is invited to join in - that includes the adults. Children love it when the teacher is one of them and plays the game. Having fun and laughing together is an important part of making and maintaining relationships.

GAMES

Mixing Games

It is beneficial for pupils to experience working with all the members of their group. This enables them to examine their thoughts, feelings and ideas and have dialogues with people who might have a different point of view or perspective to their own. It is easy and comfortable to always sit next to the same person or group of friends but mixing the pupils can encourage them to see others in a different light and be more tolerant of differences. Mixing games are a fun way to integrate the class, encourage the gender mix and anticipate behaviour problems before they arise.

Name Games

At the beginning of a new year or when somebody new enters a class, name games are important as they establish everyone's identity and help to bond the group. Using people's names is also a way of affirming each pupil in the class, of showing that they are a unique individual and someone who is special. They can be a 'spoonful of attention' for those who need it!

Game	Theme	Page
The initial game	Feelings	50
Whisper, sing, shout	Affirmation	54
Quality initials	Affirmation	61
Name clap	Caring	69
Jack in the box	Friendship	77
This is my friend	Friendship	80
Throw a name	Gender	101
Mickey Mouse	Gender	104
Action name game	Conflict Resolution	113
Call a name	Problem Solving	124
Dracula	Problem Solving	126
Trains	Problem Solving	126

Reception Class Games

Game	Theme	Page
Pass the Smile	Reception	132
Smile Swap	Reception	132
All Change	Reception	134
Magic Squeeze	Reception	134
Hello!	Reception	135
Pass the Hug	Reception	135
Hello Swap	Reception	136
The Train Song	Reception	136

Co-operative Games

One of the most important things for children to learn is how to co-operate with one another and how to get on and live and work together in a harmonious atmosphere. Circle-time activities and games will encourage pupils to look beyond their own needs , to make sure everyone is included in the games and practise the social skills needed for everyday life. These games actively encourage pupils to co-operate.

Games For Fun

CHAPTER 5 – THEMES
A Quick-Reference List

CHAPTER 5 – THEMES FOR CIRCLE-TIME

In order to make good use of the small amounts of time often allocated to pastoral care, planning a series of Circle-time themes is both practical and useful. The following are some examples of clusters of Circle-times, each free standing and purposeful on its own and each working towards a particular goal. Circles can be planned around any theme – current problems or concerns that arise from pupils, teachers and different aspects of school life.

Circle-time provides a forum in which current anxieties or ongoing concerns can be aired and discussed with the aim of providing solutions and coping strategies. Awareness of each others needs will increase through participation in Circle-time, but it is important to remember that as with any new skill, practise is essential. Pupils will come to the class with a varied social competence and experience and these individual needs will need to be taken into account. Some social skills may need more practice in order to bring about a greater degree of cohesiveness in the whole class group.

The following pages are suggestions of themes which could be used with a class. The themes have been designed to progress logically from looking at individual support systems through to assessing the needs of the group. The materials in this book provide a year's course work in PSE for the primary school teacher. They are only suggestions and are not written in tablets of stone! The Circle-time concept is one of flexibility, able to be changed to match the needs of each group of individuals. We hope you will find them helpful, both as starting points for those new to Circle-time and extensions to the repertoires of teachers already familiar with this way of working.

An Example of Using a Theme

In a small village school the boy/girl division was clear cut. The very first Circle-time revealed instantly that most boys would choose not to sit next to a girl and vice versa. One or two children always had to be 'persuaded' to fill the gap. It was not a good beginning to our circle. I organised a ..'I feel happy when ... I feel sad when' round and one of the girls was able to verbalise her unhappiness with the situation. One or two other children were also able to lend their positive voices to the discussion. We started on the gender activities and by the second week a major breakthrough occurred. The most popular boy in the class said he too thought it unreasonable and as he was such a positive role model most of the other boys could be swayed by his arguments. Led by these two children, one boy and one girl, the whole class were able to tackle the gender issue, and talk about their feelings, reluctance to mix, their views of the stereotypes and what turned out to be prejudice. They worked through the series of activities and there were many positive outcomes:

– boys and girls were able to work together collaboratively;

– organising a fair distribution of the playground for football and netball;

– the school looking at the way they lined children up in single sexes, took the register, and so forth.

Feelings

Being able to identify and recognise feelings is an essential ingredient to a successful Circle-time. During Circle-time there are lots of serious, lively discussions where feelings are discovered, explored and accepted. Pupils come to realise that if they understand themselves it will help them to understand others better.

Children learning to articulate their feelings are seen not to allow fears and worries to build up, and can gain release and relief from expression.

Expressing feelings in conflict situations is a vital element of an 'I statement' where you tell a person exactly how their behaviour effects you and at the same time keep their self-esteem intact. 'When you call out in story time it stops other children from being able to listen and I feel irritated.' Extending childrens' feelings vocabulary is a useful tool for expressing emotions and a starting point to problem solving and conflict resolution. Banks of feelings words can be recorded and made into books for use in different situations.

Children who learn to express feelings realise they are not alone, that others have the same fears and anxieties.

Feelings can be explored through games and activities and lists or books can be compiled as a reference to extend children's vocabulary.

The skills that are practised empower children by broadening their range of responses. In sharing and discussing feelings, the opportunity presents itself to talk through and see problems in a different light.

The trust and security of the circle is a powerful element, and ground rules may need to be re-stated to emphasise this.

Theme : Feelings 1 - Being Included

Warm Up Game – There's a Space on My Right

Pupils sit in a circle with one extra empty space. The person who has the empty chair on their right says, 'There's a space on my right and I would like _____ to sit in it.' The chosen person moves into the space leaving that chair empty. The game proceeds in the same way, i.e. the person who has the space on their right repeats the sentence and chooses someone. It is a useful teaching point to stop the game before everyone has had a turn or when the game stops naturally when two children keep choosing one another or the same people keep getting picked. The game can then be restarted following a discussion on fairness and the need for an agreed rule.

A Round

When I'm not chosen I feel ...

Activity

Introduce the ABC of problem solving:

Ask	How does it feel not to be chosen and what can we do about it ?
Brainstorm	Write down strategies that would be helpful. For example, in the game above it would be helpful to have a rule that states you can only be chosen once.
Choose	Write down those strategies that are fair, sensible and will work, and then choose one to try.

Conference

Ask the pupils which rules they want to add to the game to make sure everyone is included and no one is left out. They may also want to include a signal to show that someone has already been chosen, such as arms folded. Play the game again and ask the pupils if they feel there has been an improvement.

This is also an opportunity to talk to the class about how it feels to be left out in the playground and the kinds of strategies that could be employed to include everyone and to foster a caring environment.

Concluding Game – Zoom

One person starts by saying 'Zoom' turning his or her head either to the right or to the left. The person on that side passes the word 'Zoom' on to the next person and so on, until everyone has passed the 'Zoom' around the circle. Next introduce 'Eeek' (symbolic of putting the brakes on). When someone says 'Eeek' the 'Zoom' goes the opposite way round the circle.

This may be another opportunity to discuss rules and how it feels to be left out, as to begin with, everybody will want to put on the brakes and the game will be concentrated in one area.

Later children can become skilled at being responsible for keeping the game flowing and involving everyone.

Theme: Feelings 2 - Face Your Feelings

Warm Up Game – Pass the Mask

The first person makes a funny face. The next person mirrors the funny face. After he or she has copied the face, that person then moves his or her hand down across the face as if to remove the mask. He or she then makes a different funny face which is passed on to the next person. The third person first copies the face that has been shown by the second person, 'wipes' his or her face and makes a new mask. This continues until everyone in the circle has copied a funny face and made one of their own. Discuss with the pupils how they felt when they were making the faces and how they felt when someone made a face at them.

A Round

'A time when I knew how someone felt just by the way they looked was ...'

Activity

Give out the worksheet and ask pupils to look at each face, make the face themselves and then decide how they are feeling. Brainstorm ideas for each face. This will help pupils extend their vocabulary. After discussing the sheet invite children to complete it using one of the feeling words for each face. In the bottom section pupils are asked to decide how they felt yesterday, how they feel today and how they would like to feel tomorrow.

Conference

Turn to the person sitting next to you and show him or her how you were feeling yesterday.

Was it easy for them to guess just by looking at your expression?

In what other non-verbal ways do we signal our feelings to people?

Discuss other areas of body language that children could be aware of – how to pick up on non-verbal signals and what messages their body language conveys to other people.

Concluding Game – In the Manner of the Word

One pupil is asked to leave the room. The class then chooses an adjective e.g. proudly, excitedly, slowly, sadly etc. The pupil returns and instructs the class to portray an action in the manner of the chosen adjective. The player then has to guess, by looking at the body language, exactly what word was suggested.

Feelings

How are these people feeling?

_____   _____   _____

_____   _____   _____

How did you feel yesterday?   How do you feel today?   How would you like to feel tomorrow?

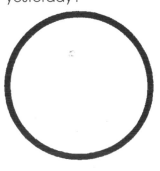 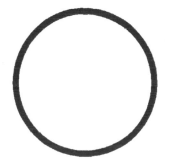 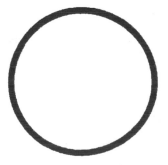

_____   _____   _____

Theme : Feelings 3 - Being New

Warm Up Game – The Initial Game

One person introduces him or herself and then says something which for example, begins with the same letter of the alphabet as their name, 'I'm Carolyn and I like Christmas.'

The person next to them continues, 'That's Carolyn and she likes Christmas and I'm Mollie and I like marzipan.' The third person then says, 'That's Carolyn and she likes Christmas. That's Mollie and she likes marzipan, and I'm Thomas and I like tigers.'

The game continues until everybody has had a turn with the whole group co-operating to help those at the end with the most to remember!

A Round

When I'm asked to do something new I feel ...

Activity

Put the chairs in a double circle so that everyone is facing somebody. Ask the pairs to tell one another about the groups they have belonged to, for example, Brownies, choir, football team, new class and so forth. When both partners have had a chance to speak and an opportunity to be listened to then the inner circle move one space to the right so that everybody has a different partner. Ask this new pair to tell each other how they felt when they joined this new group. After each pair has finished the inner circle again moves one space to the right. Ask the final pair to discuss strategies they used to help them cope with new situations. Re-form the large circle.

Conference

Take a large sheet of paper divided in three sections and elicit answers from pupils one at a time, the teacher acting as a scribe:

Groups	Feelings	Strategies
Brownies	worried	go with a friend
football	scared	smile at someone
choir	excited	introduce yourself

Encourage pupils to explore their feelings and hopefully find that they are not alone in being anxious, nervous, etc. At the end of the activity the class will have compiled a list of useful strategies.

Concluding Game – All Change

Someone stands in the middle of the circle and is the caller. The caller calls out something several of the group have in common, for example, 'Those people with black shoes,' or 'Everybody with fair hair' etc. Those pupils conforming to the call must get up and change places. The caller must sit down in one of the spaces, leaving a new caller in the middle. A list of items could be prepared or the pupils can make them up as they go along.

Theme : Feelings 4 - How Do I Feel?

Warm Up Game – Monster

The monster is in the middle of the circle and moves towards his victim slowly and menacingly (all acting of course !) If the victim can make eye contact with someone else in the circle and that person can call out their name, then they are saved and the monster advances towards the person who called out. Hence, the rescuer becomes the victim. If the monster catches you then you swap places and become the monster. This is excellent practice for making eye contact and for the whole group looking at one person.

A Round

'When I am playing a game and I lose I feel ...'

Activity

Elicit a list of feelings words from the class. Chose ten to work on for a particular session. If this activity is repeated then a different ten could be chosen. Write up the ten words and put a number by each one, for example

1. happy	2. sad	3. angry	4. shy	5. excited
6. ashamed	7. proud	8. cross	9. nervous	10. embarrassed

Divide the class into groups. Give each group a set of tag lines written on cards, to which a feeling word needs to be attached to complete the sentence. The set of cards remains face down in the centre of each group. Each person in the group takes it in turn to pick up a card, to read it out to the group and then to decide which of the ten feeling words they will use to describe how they feel about whatever is on the card. They do not tell anyone of their decision, but make a note of the number on a piece of paper. At the same time the rest of the group try to decide which feeling word that person has chosen. They also write down the number on a piece of paper. When everybody in the group has put down a number they all show each other and see if they guessed correctly. Each person in the group gets a chance to chose a card whilst the others try to guess their feelings.

Conference

The pupils might like to conference as they go along or later in the whole class group. Encourage pupils to discuss why they chose certain words. Was there a time when everyone guessed correctly? Was it difficult to imagine how other people might feel? Which was easier – choosing a feeling for yourself or for other people? How often would you have chosen the same feeling as someone else in your group?

Concluding Game – Fizz Buzz

Count around the circle starting from 1. Any number which is a multiple of 3 (6, 9 etc.) or ends in 3 (13, 23, 33 etc.) is replaced by the word 'Buzz.' Any number which is a multiple of 5 (10, 15, 20 etc.) is replaced by the word 'Fizz.' Any number which comes into both categories, such as 15, is replaced by 'Fizz Buzz.' Encourage the group to help one another – it is supposed to be fun not a maths test!

How Do I Feel?

When I have to

speak in circle-time

I feel ...

When I start

anything new

I feel ...

When I get a new

toy I feel ...

If my toy gets

broken

I feel ...

When I share my

pens with a friend

I feel ...

When someone

calls me a name

I feel ...

If I get all my

maths right

I feel ...

When people won't

let me join their

game I feel ...

These are examples of tag lines for use with this activity. Other situations can be copied from any of the rounds throughout the book.

Mollie Curry and Carolyn Bromfield, 1994
NASEN Enterprises Ltd.

Affirmation

Affirmation activities provide an opportunity for children and teachers to acknowledge and appreciate other people's qualities. In experiencing affirming activities we also learn to accept positive comments when receiving them. It *is* possible to find and recognise positive attributes in everyone.

Affirmation is a way in which we can nurture each other and enhance self-esteem so that children can believe in themselves. Affirming experiences release energy and enthusiasm for other tasks in the classroom as people who have had adequate affirming experiences in their lives can usually approach tasks or problems without fear of failing. The capacity to learn is linked to an ability or willingness to take risks.

Affirmation affects the quality of relationships in school. Adults who are able to model genuine warmth, empathy and understanding will bring these qualities to the classroom to act as role models for their pupils. Positive relationships will greatly influence changes in behaviour. Being affirmed makes it easier to see the good in others. This can reduce tensions as children find they have things in common with one another and can be 'joined' to form new friendships.

Teaching children to affirm one another and the teacher is a fundamental process in Circle-time and this theme will assist the process. The use of 'Special Person' will also be very beneficial as it provides a regular spot in the proceedings for affirming an individual. What's more, it's fun and gives a tremendous boost to the self-esteem.

Theme : Affirmation 1- Personal Shields

Warm Up Game – Whisper, Shout, Sing

To start the game, a person is chosen to call the name of someone opposite. That person repeats the action to someone else and so on. Keep this going and then start another chain where the names are whispered. When the two chains are established, start a third ... this time singing the name. If, as sometimes happens, one of the chains disappears, somebody must notice and start it up again.

A Round

My happiest day ...

Activity

This exercise is useful for the teacher to gain a view of how the pupils are feeling about themselves. It also gives an opportunity for pupils to be reflective. Use of a personal shield, with specific focus, identifies areas for discussion. Included here are two examples of shields but, as with many aspects of Circle-time, it is more meaningful to encourage the pupils to design their own and share ideas. The pupils now leave the circle to carry out the task. The shields can be drawn or written.

When the shields are complete the circle re-convenes for sharing and discussion.

Conference

Shields are displayed, one by one around the circle, with a favourite piece read out or described. Important ideas are shared and discussed.

Class 1's Cat

Someone in the circle starts off by saying: "Class 1's cat (insert your own class name or number) is an angry cat". The next person says: "Class 1's cat is a big cat". The next person thinks of an adjective beginning with 'c' to describe the cat and it goes round the circle with each person using the next letter of the alphabet. The whole class can help people who have difficult letters! Other suitable objects can be used instead of a cat.

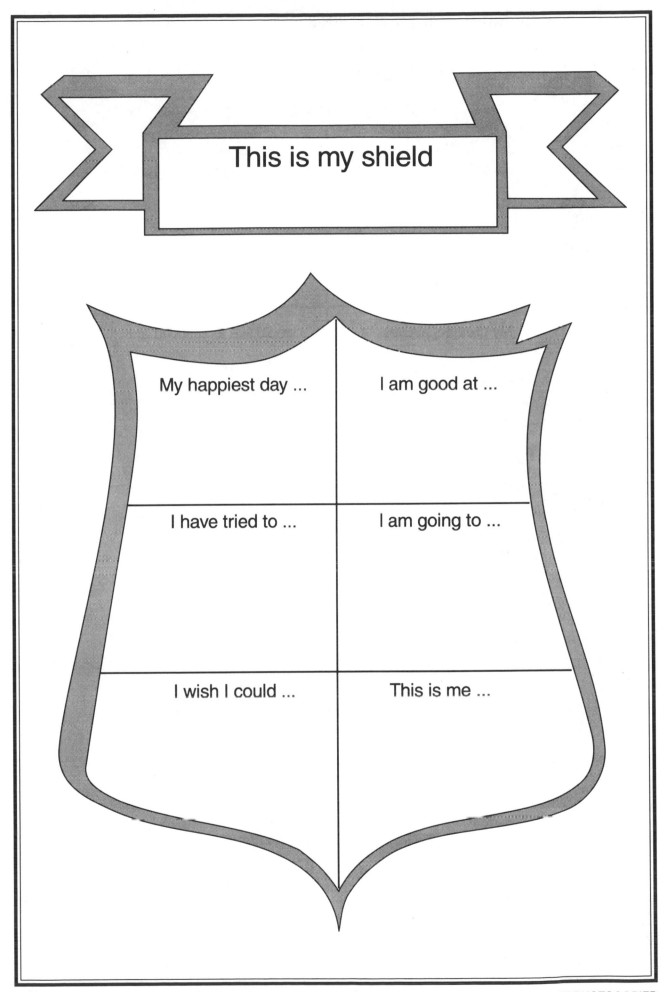

This is my shield

My happiest day ...

I am good at ...

I have tried to ...

I am going to ...

I wish I could ...

This is me ...

Mollie Curry and Carolyn Bromfield, 1994
NASEN Enterprises Ltd.

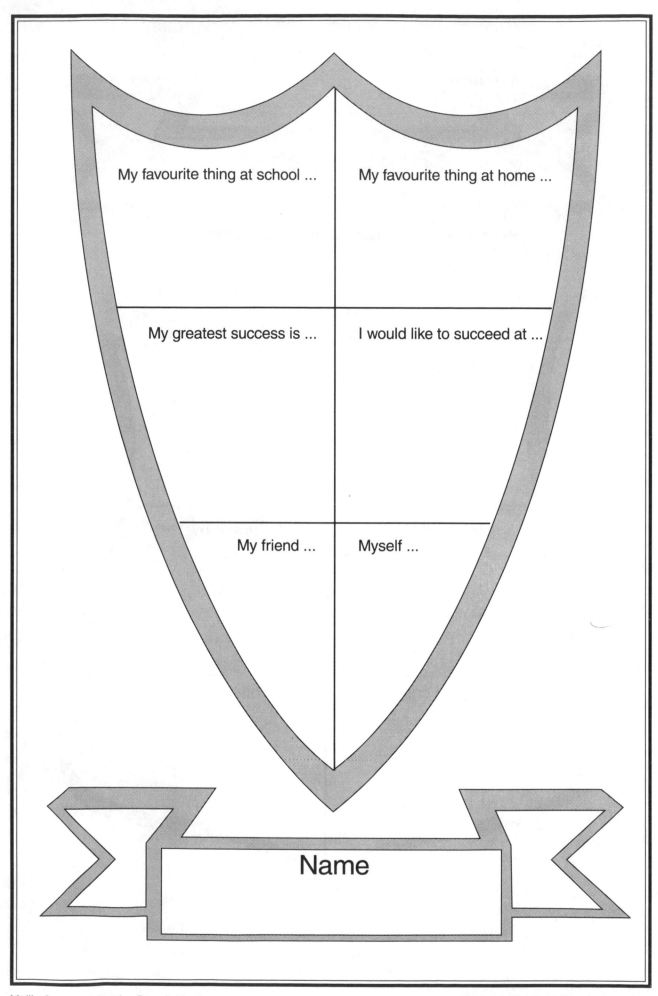

My favourite thing at school ...

My favourite thing at home ...

My greatest success is ...

I would like to succeed at ...

My friend ...

Myself ...

Name

Mollie Curry and Carolyn Bromfield, 1994
NASEN Enterprises Ltd.

Theme : Affirmation 2 - Paper Chains

Warm Up Game – The Rule of the Game

A person leaves the room. The circle decides on what is to be the rule of the game. For example, rules can be such things as, answering with your arms folded, or scratching your ear etc. The person outside comes back into the middle of the circle and asks people questions. They must listen carefully to the answer and watch the body movement to try to guess the rule of the game.

A Round

'My friends like me because ...'

Activity

Pupils with low self-esteem, often believe they are unable to do anything worthwhile. This activity illustrates we can all be good at something and at acknowledging it.

Strips of paper are given out and pupils are asked to write on each one 'I can.' Pupils are encouraged to think of all the skills and positive attributes, such as: I am good at football, I help my teacher to keep the classroom tidy; I share my pencils, etc. The strips are then glued together to form chains, and hung around the room. The chains are symbolic of the links we have with one another.

Other suggestions for paper chains are: I need help with ...; I enjoy ...; I am good at ...; I hope I can....

Conference

The circle is reformed and the completed chains are shown. Pupils are encouraged to read some out loud. They are then displayed around the room or taken home.

Concluding Game – Who's Missing?

One person is chosen to leave the room, or turn around and close their eyes. The teacher points to somebody and they have to move to another place in the circle. The chosen person rejoins the circle and has to guess who has moved. As the children become more skilled more people can be moved in one go. This is a good game for testing observation and memory.

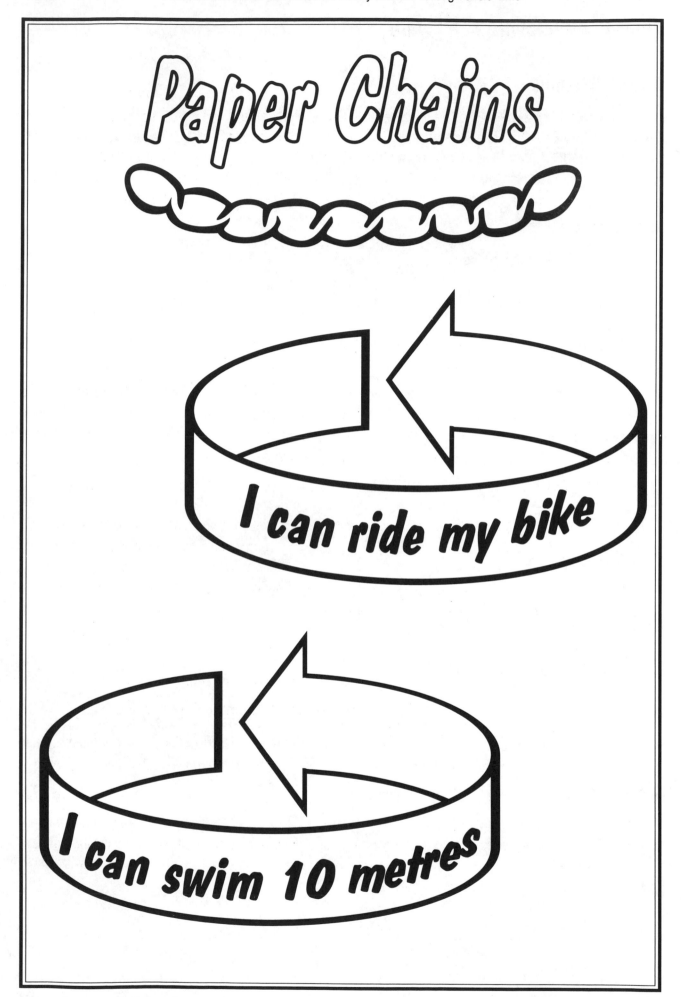

Paper Chains

I can ride my bike

I can swim 10 metres

Mollie Curry and Carolyn Bromfield, 1994
NASEN Enterprises Ltd.

Theme : Affirmation 3 - If I Were

Warm Up Game – I Sit

A spare chair is brought into the circle. The people either side of the empty space try to sit on the chair. The one who is successful says, 'I sit.' The person next to them moves up one seat and says 'in the woods.' The third person moves up one seat and says, 'And I choose _____ to sit next to me.' A space is now created in another part of the circle and the game continues. This game gives the opportunity for a lot of children to move around the circle and for every child to be affirmed as their name is called out when they are chosen.

A Round

'My friends like me because ...'

Activity

This is a lighthearted approach to affirming the positive in everyone. Give out the worksheets and then get the pupils to reflect on their own positive attributes. What kind of a person are they? Are they strong, quick, cuddly, reliable, agile, intelligent, attractive? They may need a partner to help them decide. When they have done this they need to choose a friend and sit on the opposite side of the circle to their friend.

Now ask the pupils to think of their attributes and think about what kind of animal, insect, plant, they might be. For example, if they think they are strong yet sensitive, they might choose to be a gorilla! If they think they are busy and productive, they might chose to be a bee! Then they have to think of the attributes their friend has and think what kind of an animal, insect or plant they might be.

Conference

Pupils sit next to their friends again and compare categories.

Were there any similarities? Did your friend see you as 'an owl' (or whatever) too?

Ask your friend why they chose certain answers – what attributes do they think you have?

Were there any surprises? Did you know this is how other people saw you?

Concluding Game – Postman

One pupil, who is the postman, gives each person in the circle a number. The postman then calls out two numbers and those pupils have to change places. The postman tries to sit in one of the spaces and the person who is left in the middle of the circle is the new postman.

If I Were ....

Write or draw your answers in the spaces.

If I were an animal I would be a ... My friend would be a ...	If I were a plant I would be a ... My friend would be a ...
If I were a colour I would be ... My friend would be ...	If I were an insect I would be ... My friend would be a ...
If I were a bird I would be a ... My friend would be a ...	If I were a vehicle I would be ... My friend would be a ...
If I were a fish I would be ... My friend would be ...	If I were a piece of furniture I would be ... My friend would be ...
My favourite is ...	

Theme : Affirmation 4 - Affirmation Flowers

Warm Up Game – Quality Initials

One person introduces him or herself, putting a descriptive word in front of their name that starts with the same letter of the alphabet e.g. 'Happy Hamid,' 'Marvellous Mario.'

This continues with each pupil introducing him or herself in turn – 'Hello I'm Artistic Andrew,' and so on.

A Round

'When I'm left out I feel ...'

Activity

This activity is an opportunity for pupils and teacher to affirm one another and to experience how that feels. Organise the class into small groups of five or six, and give everyone a flower, asking them to write their name. Each person passes his or her flower one place to the right. That person then writes a positive comment (an affirmation) about the person named in the centre of the flower. Every one in the group contributes to each flower, (see sample). It is possible to include an extra petal or a leaf on which a self-affirmation can be written. When the task is complete, the circle re-convenes.

Older pupils can make their own flower centre and petals and give them to one another. Centres can be also pinned to the wall and petals added throughout the day. This could be a whole class activity.

Conference

Affirmation flowers are displayed, one by one, around the circle and pupils are encouraged to read out their favourite affirmation.

Concluding Game – Sleepmaker

One person stands with their back to the group, whilst a 'sleepmaker' is chosen. The person standing then moves into the centre of the circle and tries to discover who is the 'sleepmaker.' The 'sleepmaker' has to send people to sleep by winking at them but must do so without being detected. This game can have a calming effect. This game is also known as 'Wink Murder' which older pupils enjoy. (Some classes may need the rule to 'die' quietly!)

Mollie Curry and Carolyn Bromfield, 1994
NASEN Enterprises Ltd.

Caring

Caring as part of the ethos in any class is a desirable goal. The following Circle-time theme examines the notion of care and respect for others. By increasing awareness and skill levels of children it is possible to build a community in which mutual well being is the norm. The topics provide a framework for a model and explore the skills and strategies needed to maintain such a community. Ideas and solutions on *how* we care are identified and practised.

This theme encourages children to appreciate other people and helps to shape attitudes. The ideal is for every child to be able to perceive and respond to the needs of others, and for concern to be expressed within an atmosphere of trust and security.

Caring is all about being sensitive to the needs of others, about developing an awareness of others, and this includes the teacher. Learning to care is helped by being able to make connections and understanding the effect of an individual's actions - both positive and negative. Teachers' modelling of genuine care and warmth will be a key to fostering this in their pupils.

Theme : Caring 1 – Caring Hands Tree

Warm-up Game – This is a Handshake

The first person turns to the pupil on his or her right, shakes hands and says, 'This is a handshake.' The receiver says, ' What is it?' and the first person responds, 'A handshake'. This action is passed round the circle. It is fun to pass handshakes in opposite directions at the same time and watch what happens when they meet. You can also pass round other actions such as a 'pat on the back' or a hug.

A Round

'When people care about me I feel ...'

Activity – Caring Hands Tree; Hurtful Hands Tree

Draw round children's hands on a large sheet of paper. Join up the hands, and add a trunk to form a tree. Using the magic microphone go round the circle and ask for one helpful, kind, caring thing that our hands can do. Write the words on the hands. Alternatively pupils could draw round their own hands and write about something helpful they have done this week.

Repeat the exercise but this time talking about the unkind, hurtful things that hands can do.

Conference

Elicit and record the feelings:

When people are kind I feel ...	When people hurt me I feel ...

Concluding Game – Electric Squeeze

Children hold hands. One person gently squeezes the person to his or her left and that person squeezes the hand on their left and so on until the squeeze has passed right round the circle. The idea is for the children to watch in silence as the squeeze moves round the circle. Explain that a squeeze is like 'a cuddle with your hands' – it is a caring, gentle action, not one that hurts. This activity helps to calm the children down and reunite the group.

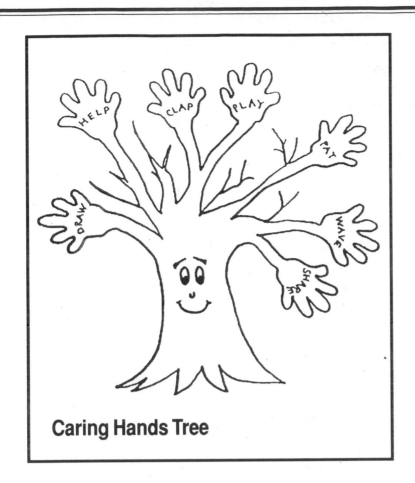

Caring Hands Tree

Hurtful Hands Tree

Mollie Curry and Carolyn Bromfield, 1994
NASEN Enterprises Ltd.

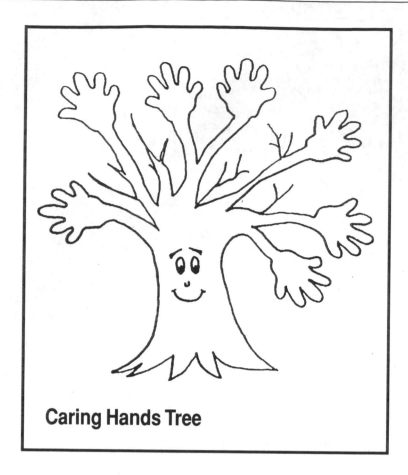

Caring Hands Tree

Hurtful Hands Tree

Mollie Curry and Carolyn Bromfield, 1994
NASEN Enterprises Ltd.

Theme : Caring 2 - Wishes And Hopes

Warm Up Game – Farmyard

Choose four animals and give each person in the circle the name of one animal. For example : sheep, duck, horse, cow, sheep, duck, horse, cow etc. The name of one animal is called out and those people change places. If 'Farmyard' is called everyone changes places.

A Round

'If I could have any wish in the world I would wish for ...'

Activity

This activity encourages pupils to think of other people as well as an opportunity for self-reflection. It is an individual task and allows for confidentiality. Pupils are asked to complete the following sections: Wishes and hopes for myself are ...; Wishes and hopes for my family are ...; Wishes and hopes for the world are ...; When the task is finished, the circle re-convenes.

Conference

Elicit from the pupils the sections that were easy to complete, or those that were more difficult, and invite pupils to share if they wish. The finished strips are then stapled or stuck together and can be displayed on the painted branch of a tree. This is in fact an idea from Japan, where hopes for the future are transported on the breeze!

Concluding Game – Detective

One person goes out of the room while the rest of the class picks a leader. The person comes back and stands in the middle of the circle. Everyone copies the actions of the leader such as, tapping the head, patting the knees, clapping hands, whilst the detective has to try to spot the leader.

Wishes
and
Hopes

I wish ....

I wish ....

For
Myself

I hope ....

For My
Family

Wishes and hopes for myself and my family
and on the back of the strip, for the world.

Mollie Curry and Carolyn Bromfield, 1994
NASEN Enterprises Ltd.

Theme : Caring 3 – My Special Thing

Warm Up Game – Name Clap

Everybody claps a rhythm together and then says the name of each person going round the circle. For example: clap knees (twice); clap hands (twice); say person's name. 'Knees, hands, Jo!' 'Knees, hands, Ahmid!'

A variation on this game (as well as changing the rhythms) is to bounce the name around the circle. Everybody joins in the claps, but only one person says a name, everybody claps again and the named person says someone else's name.

This is a 'spoonful of attention' for every pupil.

A Round

'My favourite thing is ...'

Activity

Ask the pupils to bring something special to school to share. Obviously they must ask their parents permission and it has to be portable and something that is not too precious. This is an occasion for pupils to share something of themselves with the whole class and gives the opportunity for information gathering as pupils ask questions about each object. Pupils can be encouraged to think of three attributes that describe their object (for example, beautiful, practical, cuddly) and share these with a friend. Their friend can decide whether those attributes can also be related to the pupil!

Next tell the pupils to put the object behind their back and pretend that it is lost. How do they feel? Pupils then place their object back in front of them and are told it has been found again. How do they feel now? Repeat this operation several times and see if the feelings change.

Conference

Ask: Where do you keep special things in this class?

How can we keep things safe?

Do we need a rule?

How do we feel if people touch things that belong to us without our permission?

Concluding Game – Pass the Bean Bag

Everybody starts with a bean bag. If you haven't got bean bags anything will do, even a shoe! The idea is to pass your bean bag to the person on your right, clap your hands, and receive a bean bag from the person on your left. This works best if the whole group practises a rhythm on the spot before you start passing e.g. put down, clap, pick up. You will need to put down with your left hand and pick up with your right hand (transferring in between.)

Somehow this game always ends up with someone having a pile of bean bags in front of them – but it doesn't matter, it's all great fun!

Theme : Caring 4 – Warm Fuzzies

Warm Up Game – Pirate's Treasure

The pirate sits in the centre of the circle and is blindfolded with his treasure (a bunch of keys or something else that is noisy) in front of him. Someone is chosen to try to take the treasure without the pirate hearing. If the pirate hears someone they are to point in the direction of that person and if they are correct that person has to sit down and someone else is chosen. If they manage to steal the treasure then they can choose to be the pirate or nominate someone else.

This is a good game for co-operative concentration as the whole group are encouraged to sit in silence to assist the pirate.

A Round

Something nice that happened to me this week ...

Activity – Warm Fuzzies and Cold Pricklies

Read the story of *The Original Warm Fuzzy Tale* by Claude Steiner (Jalmar Press) to the class. This enchanting story is about a make-believe land where everybody is born with a bag full of 'warm fuzzies'. Any time you wanted to feel happy all you had to do was reach into the bag and take out a 'warm fuzzy' or ask someone else to give you one of theirs. The story also includes a wicked witch who devises a plan to deprive people of their good feelings and replace them with 'cold pricklies' (ugh!). Fortunately the story has a happy ending.

Tell each child to imagine that they have their draw string bag full of 'warm fuzzies' in front of them and that they are to take one out and put it on their shoulder and let it melt into their body. Mime the lovely warm glow that comes from within when something pleasant happens to you and let the children 'feel' that sensation.

Discuss with the children what exactly is meant by the term 'warm fuzzy' as, initially, the children might take it to be the little soft creatures in the story or things that literally make you warm such as a fire. Warm fuzzies are things that make you feel good e.g. smiles, hugs, saying 'please' and 'thank you,' sharing, having friends. Cold pricklies are the opposite.

Working in groups children can brainstorm lists of warm fuzzies and cold pricklies. They can then go on to make the warm fuzzy mobiles using a coat hanger, card, string and felt tips to decorate the class and serve as a creative reminder.

Conference

What does it feel like when you receive a 'warm fuzzy'?
Share some experiences of warm fuzzies.
What does it feel like when you receive a 'cold prickly'?

If you are going to share experience of cold pricklies then make sure children understand the confidentiality rule that we do not name individuals when talking about anything negative. Children can say something like, 'I had a cold prickly yesterday when someone called me a name.' When incidents of inappropriate behaviour occur following this Circle-time the teacher can ask 'Is that a warm fuzzy?' or 'If you continue to do that will you get a warm fuzzy or a cold prickly?' This is a useful tool for self-correction.

Concluding Game – Statues

One person directs the group by giving an instruction e.g. 'Jump up and down!'   'Touch your nose!' 'Clap your hands!' At some point they say 'Stop' and all the people must 'freeze' as they are into statues. The 'director' tries to make people 'unfreeze' by making them laugh (without touching them). The first person to unfreeze becomes the new 'director' and the game begins again.

wave   tidy up   come and join
                                  our game

        clap

    smile   hugs   cuddles
            say hello

    share books   help someone
                            when they are hurt

        play together

say please and thank you

            well done   praise

do you need some help?

        make a card   make a present·

I like you   shake hands

        hold the door open

Mollie Curry and Carolyn Bromfield, 1994
NASEN Enterprises Ltd.

kicking   biting   smacking

being nasty   hurting someone

thumping   fights   pushing

answering back   punching

leaving litter about   telling tales

Cold Pricklies

letting someone else take the blame

glaring   showing off

throwing things   calling people names

pinching

destroying a model

hurting an animal   bully

Mollie Curry and Carolyn Bromfield, 1994
NASEN Enterprises Ltd.

Making a Mobile

Mollie Curry and Carolyn Bromfield, 1994
NASEN Enterprises Ltd.

Friendships

The ability to communicate effectively with others is a large part of being able to function interpersonally and an important task of childhood learning is to form positive relationships. Children need to understand how friendships are developed and maintained and in order for this to happen they must also acquire the ability to look at things from another person's point of view.

Engendering friendships and relationships enables both teachers and pupils to gain better insight into one another and looking at friendship structures allows exploration by the group of ways in which they are alike and ways in which they differ.

Friends play an important part in every child's life and each new relationship enlarges a child's outlook on the world. Learning about others also affords the child the opportunity to learn more about themselves. Through the feedback that we receive from interactions with others we form a picture of how others see us. The more positive the interaction the more positive the view. The social and emotional climate of the classroom will be determined by the beliefs and attitudes individuals have of themselves.

Friendship can be 'helped along' by Circle-time activities with support built into the process. This enables vulnerable children to be helped by their peers when adults are not readily available. Often a potential outburst can be averted by a calm word from a sensitive friend.

Circle-time work on friendship raises the skill level and awareness of everyone. The knowledge and insight can then in turn serve as a resource, as a point of reference when appropriate.

Theme: Friendship 1 – This Is My Friend

Warm Up Game – Prueey

One player is the 'prueey.' The other pupils wander around the classroom with their eyes closed bumping into people as they move around. When one pupil bumps into another they say 'Prueey, Prueey' and the other pupil replies 'Prueey, Prueey.' The real Prueey does not speak and so the call of 'Prueey' is not responded to. When this happens, the pupils link arms so that there are now two pupils who are the Prueey, both of them not being able to speak but with their eyes open. The chain of Prueeys becomes longer and longer until the whole class is linked together.

A Round

When I first started school I made friends with (names). I liked them because ...

Activity

After generating ideas from the 'round' above discuss the qualities of a friend.

Brainstorm ideas for, 'A friend is someone who ... '

In pairs discuss, 'Friends don't ... '

Back in the large circle generate a second list. Give out worksheet and ask pupils to draw a picture of their friend and complete the sentence, 'A friend is someone who ... ' They can chose the attributes that they consider to be most important.

Conference

Even when you are friends with someone, he or she may do things which you do not like. Children need to be given strategies to deal with these situations and the opportunity to practise them in the safety of the circle. Situations such as when a friend uses your felt-tips without asking, what do you do that will not lead to a confrontation and will keep their self-esteem intact? One strategy to teach children is for them to say, 'I like you but I don't like it when (name the behaviour).'

For example, 'I like you but I don't like it when you use my felt-tips without asking.'

Ask for behaviours which annoy or upset pupils and get them to act out little scenes in which they can practise this strategy. Do not allow anybody to be personally named – this activity concentrates solely on the behaviour not the individual. We very much want to stress, 'We like you, but we don't like what you are doing.'

Concluding Game – People to people

Everyone finds a friend except one person who is the caller in the middle of the circle. The caller shouts out instructions to the pairs such as : 'Hand to knee!', 'Back to back!', 'Shoulder to shoulder!' and the pairs follow them. After a while, the caller shouts 'People to people!' and everyone has to find a different partner. The caller also finds a partner which will leave a new caller in the middle of the circle.

Name_____

This is my friend _____

A friend is someone who ....

_____

_____

_____

_____

Theme : Friendship 2 – Friendship Questionnaire

Warm Up Game – Jack in the Box

The first person stands up and says his or her name, 'I'm Claus.' Claus then introduces the two people on his left, starting with the one next to him. 'This is Lara and this is Hassina.' When each person is named they stand up and then sit down quickly – hence the jack-in-the-box effect. The second person then stands up, introduces herself and the two people on her left, 'I'm Lara. This is Hassina and this is Sam.' When they hear their name they quickly stand up and then sit down.

A Round

'A good friend is someone who ...'

Activity – Friendship

Give each pupil a copy of the friendship questionnaire and ask them to read the questions and tick the appropriate answers. Stress that there are no right or wrong answers and that no one will be asked to share with the group unless they wish to do so. This will encourage children to answer truthfully and allow them to get more from the exercise. Younger children might need the questions read to them.

Conference

Once the questionnaire has been completed, each situation can be discussed with pupils offering, on a voluntary basis, suggestions as to what they would have done or what they think should be done. They may also be able to offer alternative suggestions and discuss why people do not always do what they think they ought to.

Concluding Game – Chinese Fingers

Pupils sit in circle with everyone looking at the back of the person to their left. Someone starts off by drawing, with their fingers, an object on the back of the person in front. That person then draws what he or she felt on the person in front of him or her. Just like 'Chinese Whispers,' the drawn object passes round the whole group until it reaches the person who started. They then tell the group what the object was and others discuss what they thought had been drawn on their backs. Younger children might enjoy 'drawing' numbers or letters.

Friendship Questionnaire

Tick the answer you think you would do in each situation

A. Your friend comes to your house and shows you their new jeans.

Do you say:
1. 'You look great!'
2. 'They don't suit you!'
3. 'You like the jeans but you think they look nicer in their shell suit!'

B. Your best friend copies you in a spelling test.

Do you:
1. tell them off?
2. tell them they are not your best friend?
3. tell teacher?
4. say that you are pleased you were able to be helpful?

C. A new class member is finding it hard to settle and looks more and more unhappy every day.

Do you:
1. ignore them?
2. ask them to join in with your friends?
3. leave your own friends and look after the new person?

D. No one will play with you following a playground argument.

Do you:
1. stay on your own until its forgotten?
2. think of ways of getting back at them?
3. go and tell your friends you are sorry?
4. tell your teacher?
5. play with someone in another class?

E. You and your friends usually give each other a birthday present but this year they forgot your birthday.

Do you:
1. give them your present anyway?
2. don't give them anything?
3. give them something very small?

F. A friend does not have a snack.

Do you:
1. share yours equally?
2. eat all the snack yourself?
3. give them a tiny part?

Mollie Curry and Carolyn Bromfield, 1994
NASEN Enterprises Ltd.

Friendship Questionnaire

G. You accidentally break your friend's calculator.

Do you:
1. say sorry?
2. say it was already broken?
3. offer to replace it?

H. Your friend is asked to show round some important visitors.

Do you:
1. say 'Lucky you!' but actually feel jealous?
2. hope they are ill and can't do it?
3. say you are pleased?
4. tell everyone they are teacher's pet?

I. You see a friend in your class teasing a younger child.

Do you:
1. walk away and pretend you haven't noticed?
2. interfere and stop it?
3. tell your teacher?

J. You see a girl in your class take some money from the teacher's desk.

Do you:
1. tell them quietly to put it back?
2. ignore it as its nothing to do with you?
3. tell the teacher?

K. Your friend has to wear glasses but the pair that he or she has chosen are not very smart.

Other children begin to make unkind comments.

Do you:
1. join in the fun – he or she will have to learn to put up with the teasing?
2. walk away embarrassed?
3. say you like them and you're glad they will be able to see better now?
4. invite your friend to go with you to another part of the playground?

Mollie Curry and Carolyn Bromfield, 1994
NASEN Enterprises Ltd.

Theme : Friendship 3 – Portrait Of A Friend

Warm Up Game – This is My Friend

Each pupil talks to the person next to them for a few minutes and finds out three things about them, (their favourite colour, their hobby, something they are proud of, etc) When they have both exchanged information, each pair goes and finds another pair and introduces their friend. 'This is Anna. Her favourite colour is red. She likes white chocolate and is good at swimming.' This game requires concentration and good listening skills.

A Round

The thing I look for in a friend is ...

Activity

Discuss with a partner the attributes that make you a good friend. Starting with a tag-line can be helpful, for example 'Friends like me because ...!' Make a list of the attributes. Give out the worksheet and ask pupils to design a poster advertising themselves as a friend.

Conference

Share the finished posters and look at the common attributes people used to describe themselves. What were the most popular? Discuss the sorts of things that friends might do for one another and set up a task sheet from ideas generated to be completed by pupils when other school work is finished during the week and before the next Circle-time. Encourage every pupil to complete the tasks (see sample sheet).

Concluding Game – Whales, Winkles and Crabs

Pupils are called 'whales,' 'winkles' or 'crabs,' going round the circle. When one of these groups are called 'into the sea' they go out through a gap in the circle and run clockwise round the outside. If 'Fast tide' is called, they move quickly and if 'Slow tide' is called, they move slowly. 'Trawlers' means that they have to move on their hands and knees (to avoid the nets), and 'Tide turns,' causes the group to move in the opposite direction. When 'Tide in' is called, the runners must complete the circuit and return to their seats through the gap in the circle. No overtaking is allowed; it is not a race and group members must look after one another.

If you feel brave, then more than one group may be called at a time!

This is the portrait of a friend

My name is _____

Friends like me because .....

_____

_____

_____

_____

Mollie Curry and Carolyn Bromfield, 1994
NAEN Enterprises Ltd.

Friendship Task Sheet

**Tick off each task as you complete it. The tasks can be done
in any order.**

1. Make a card for a friend.

2. Write a five line friendship poem.
   Friends are:
   1st line – 1 attribute;
   2nd line – 1 attribute;
   3rd line – 1 attribute;
   4th line – 1 attribute;
   5th line – a friend's name.

3. Write or draw about a friendly deed you have done this week.

4. Write a letter to a penfriend and describe yourself.

5. Read a story about friends and their adventures.

6. Write a menu for a party for your friends.

I have finished all the tasks. Signed: _____

The task I enjoyed most was _____

because _____

Mollie Curry and Carolyn Bromfield, 1994
NASEN Enterprises Ltd.

Theme : Friendship 4 – Being Helpful

Warm Up Game – What are you doing?

One player starts by miming an action (brushing hair, ironing, washing hands etc). The whole group copies the mime. When they have copied the action once, the person next to the mimer says, 'What are you doing?' The mimer replies by saying something totally inappropriate such as 'I'm washing my elephant.' On hearing this, the whole group now copies the new mime suggested. The next person round the circle repeats the process by asking, 'What are you doing?' Whilst miming one action, he or she replies with another. The whole group copies the new action and this continues until everybody has suggested a mime. This is a fun activity, but can lead to questions about helpful and unhelpful information and how it feels when you know people are not being honest or truthful.

A Round

'When I need help I wish others would ...'

Activity

Discuss : Is it hard to ask for help? What makes it easier? Who do we go to when we need help in school? How can we signal a friend? What are non-verbal signals?

Work in pairs: A person who helped me a lot is ...
One thing I could help someone else with is ...
Work in fours: Discuss and complete the 'Being helpful' chart. It might need to be enlarged.

Before the small groups start the activity there may need to be some discussions about group work and the formulation of some rules, such as:

1. We take turns to talk.
2. We listen to the person who is speaking.
3. Each person in the group gets a turn to be scribe (one for each section).
4. We value others points of view.
5. Only positive comments are allowed.

Conference

Share the information collected on the charts. Pupils take it in turns to report back for their group. Teacher can act as the scribe and collect a list of ways in which children can be helpful in school. A book could be started in which all the helpful deeds for a week are noted down by the teacher and pupils – these could then be shared at the end of the week or during a celebration assembly. Certificates could be awarded to children for acts of kindness.

Concluding Game – Shunting

One person stands in the middle of the circle and says ' Shunt to the right,' and everybody moves to their right until a new order is called. 'Shunt to the left and everybody changes direction and moves to the left. At the instruction 'All change' everybody swaps seats and the person in the middle must find a seat leaving a new caller in the middle. The instructions can be given in any order but care must be taken to play the game at such a speed that allows all children to participate safely. Everybody in the group is responsible for one another.

Friendship : Being Helpful

Who helps us?	What do we do to help others?
How do we feel when they help us?	**How do we feel when we help others?**

Co-operation

To day there is a growing demand for true collaborative group work in primary classrooms, and for a highly developed skill of co-operation. This 'co-operative classroom' will not happen without planning and preparation from the teacher. Children will need to be taught the necessary social skills to enable them to work co-operatively.

Co-operation can be seen when pupils are working peacefully together, on a task for a joint outcome. Each group is contributing to work or each group member donates to the work of the group.

Co-operative games will enhance group cohesion and give the opportunity for co-operation in a fun way. This can be followed up by eliciting how the game worked, or 'unpicking' how or where it went wrong, what were the strengths and weaknesses and most important of all how it felt.

Circle-time activities and games are structured to ensure that there are no winners or losers and that each child's participation is necessary for the group to succeed.

This information about co-operative skills and the learning that follows can then be applied to academic tasks in the classroom.

Co-operation needs practise and fine tuning. For some groups or individuals the learning needs to be clearly explained, or connections made between outcomes.

The following Circle-time theme gives opportunity for co-operation to be experienced and encourages pupils to focus on the aspects mentioned above. Some pupils need help and guidance in this important part of learning as they may not acquire the skills without some direct intervention.

Theme : Co-operation 1 – Co-operation Pictures

Warm Up Game – Puzzle Game

Give out pieces of the puzzles. To make the puzzles, draw pictures on circles of card and cut each circle into three. Pictures from magazines could also be used and pupils could be encouraged to make their own. Give each person a piece of a puzzle. Each piece needs two others to go with it to complete the whole. We need to co-operate with others to complete this task. When the three people have found one another and completed the puzzle, they sit down together on the edge of the circle.

A Round

'I think it is important to co-operate with others because ...'

Activity

Included with this activity are a set of five pictures (see pages 88 to 92) which need to be cut into pieces along the lines indicated. The class should be divided into groups of five and each group needs a set of pictures. For each set, mark five envelopes A to E and put the appropriate pieces in each envelope. Give each group one set of pictures, with each child having one envelope. Spare children can act as observers. Tell the children that the envelopes are not to be opened until you give the signal.

Give the following instructions :

1. Each of you has an envelope containing pieces of a puzzle, but the pieces in your envelope do not fit together to make a complete picture. The task of the group is to make five identical pictures, one in front of each of you. The task will not be complete until everyone has a whole picture in front of them, so you will need to help one another.

2. You are not allowed to take the pieces you want. You are not allowed to ask for the pieces you want. How are you going to complete your puzzle? (After discussion hopefully someone will come up with the solution) – You are only allowed to give pieces to other people and each piece must be given to a specific person.

3. No one may speak and non-verbal communication is forbidden, such as hand signals or longing glances, are forbidden. When everybody has understood the instructions then give the signal to start.

Conference

Ask:
1. How did you feel during the activity?
2. Did you find it hard not to talk?
3. Did you cheat?
4. Did you find the other members of the group co-operated with one another?

Concluding Game – Partner Balances

Pupils find a partner of equal height and size. Partners sit back to back with elbows interlinked, legs outstretched. They try to stand up helping one another. Couples join to make a four and try the same thing. Next, partners can sit facing one another with legs outstretched, feet touching. They hold hands and try to pull each other up to a standing position.

Co-operative Picture Puzzles

Mollie Curry and Carolyn Bromfield, 1994
NASEN Enterprises Ltd.

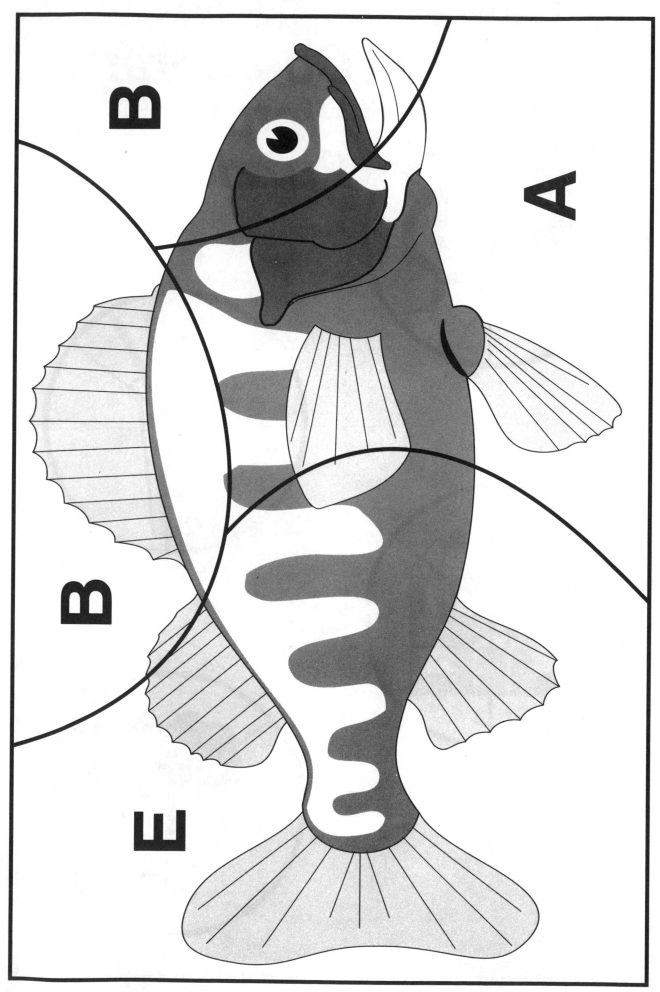

Mollie Curry and Carolyn Bromfield, 1994
NASEN Enterprises Ltd.

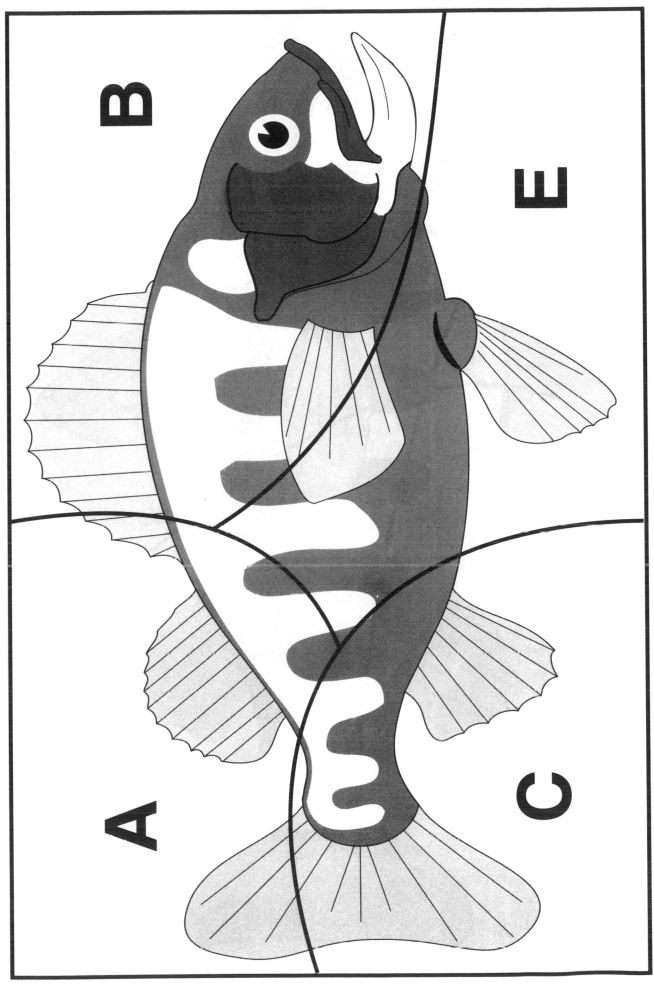

Mollie Curry and Carolyn Bromfield, 1994
NASEN Enterprises Ltd.

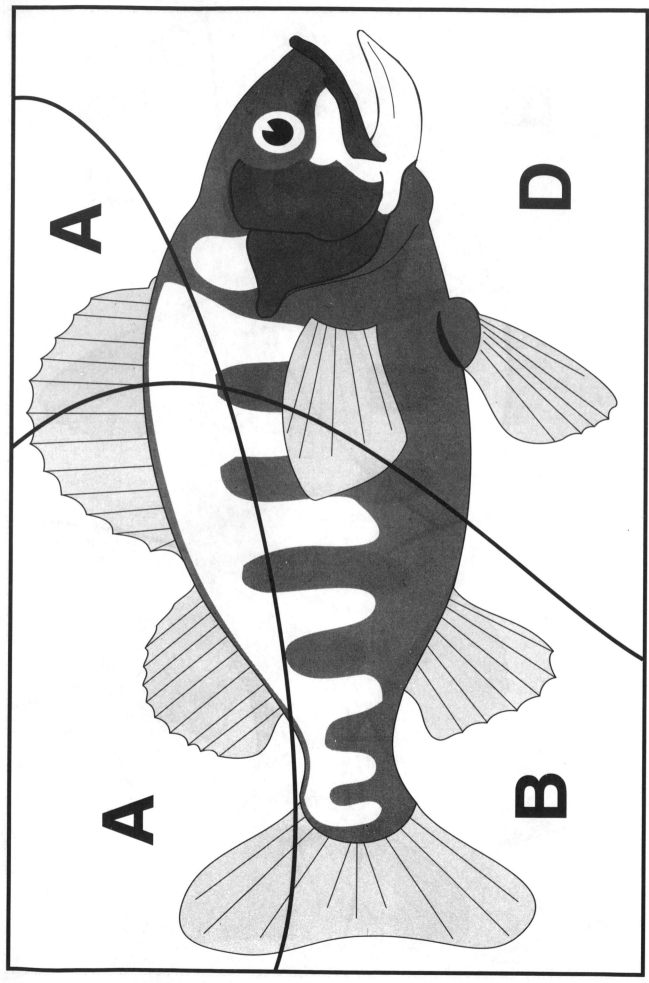

Mollie Curry and Carolyn Bromfield, 1994
NASEN Enterprises Ltd.

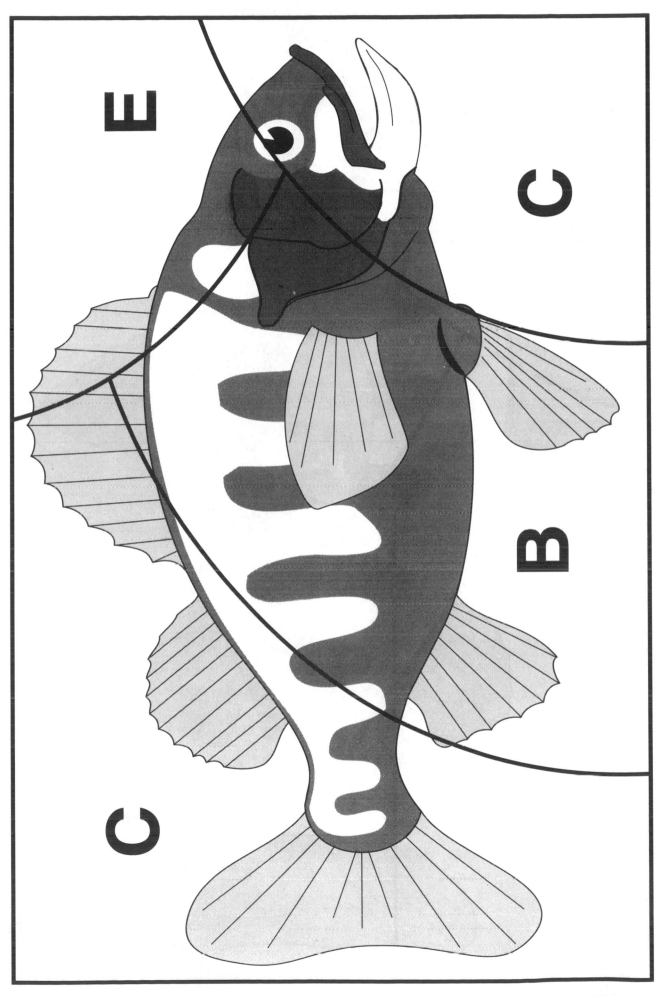

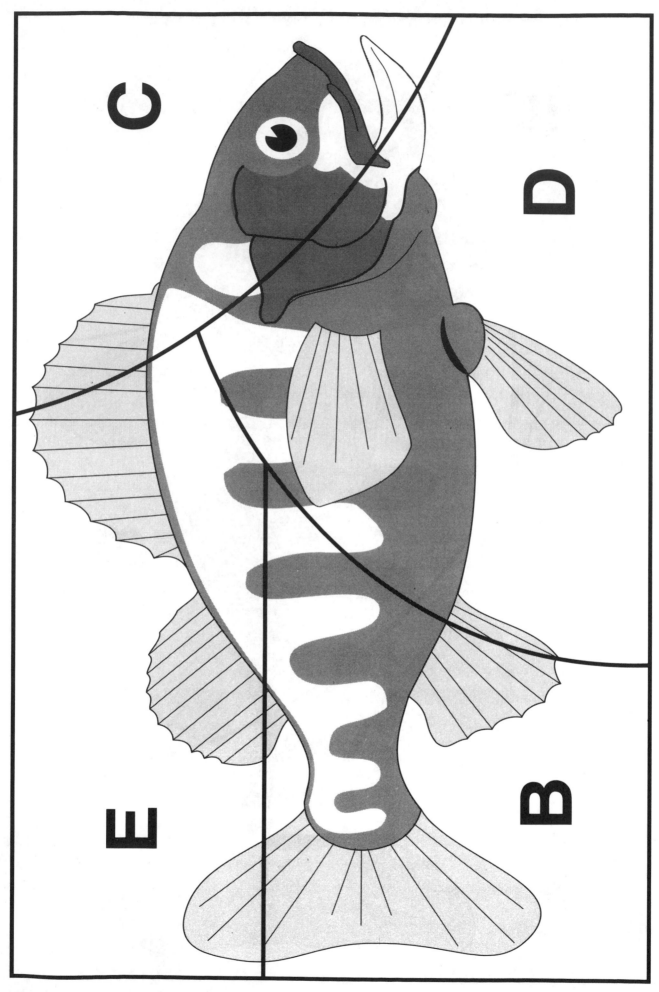

Mollie Curry and Carolyn Bromfield, 1994
NASEN Enterprises Ltd.

Theme : Co-operation 2 – People Hunt

Warm Up Game – Find the Colour

Pupils choose a colour. They are then asked to move around the circle and find other pupils who have chosen the same colour. They must do all of this without speaking. Pointing at an object with the same colour is not permitted. They must communicate their choice by miming their colour in whatever way seems appropriate. When two pupils have found one another they must continue until they think they have found everybody in their group. At the end the teacher asks each group what colour they are – are any members in the wrong group? If anyone is in the wrong group ask how the misunderstandings occurred. Are there any children who could not find anybody else who had made the same choice – how did they feel? This game can raise all sorts of questions about membership of minority and majority groups.

A Round

'When I am part of a group I feel ...'

Activity

Give out worksheets to each pupil and tell them to walk round the circle and hunt for people who can answer their questions. (The questions can be asked in any order). If they find a pupil who answers 'Yes' to one of their questions he or she is asked to sign the paper. Every signature obtained on the worksheet must be different and they are not allowed to sign their own sheet. This is not a competitive activity and there is not a prize for finishing first! Pupils should be encouraged to share experiences fully before moving on to the next question.

Conference

- Did anyone find out anything about someone that they didn't know before?
- What interesting thing did they find out about someone in the class?
- What did they find they had in common with someone else?
- Did they find any questions difficult to answer?
- Was it easy to share their feelings?
- Could they complete the people hunt? If not what were the problems?

Concluding Game – Knots

Everyone in the circle stands with their arms stretched out in front of them. With their eyes closed, they slowly walk towards the centre of the circle. They then hold hands with two other people. When everybody is linked, the whole group opens its eyes and attempts to untangle themselves, without letting go of the hands. The group must work together to solve the problem. The group may end up in one big circle, or two smaller circles or circles that are entwined.

A People Hunt

Find someone who ...

1. Has the same colour eyes. _____

2. Has the same colour socks. _____

3. Is taller than you. _____

4. Likes sweets. _____

5. Has a pet. _____

6. Has curly hair. _____

7. Can sing, 'Baa, baa, black sheep'. _____

8. Can swim. _____

9. Can count to 20. _____

10. Is 6 or older. _____

11. Can play a musical instrument. _____

12. Wears glasses. _____

Mollie Curry and Carolyn Bromfield, 1994
NASEN Enterprises Ltd.

A People Hunt – 2

Find someone who ...

1. Has the same colour hair as you.   _____

2. Has an interesting hobby.   _____

3. Felt happy recently (share the reason).   _____

4. Felt sad recently (ask what happened).   _____

5. Can play a musical instrument.   _____

6. Can do an impression of someone famous.   _____

7. Learnt something new recently.   _____

8. Has been kind to someone recently.   _____

9. Was not chosen for something (ask how they felt). _____

10. Felt scared recently (share it).   _____

11. Can say some foreign words.   _____

12. Has been abroad for a holiday.   _____

13. Has a pet.   _____

14. Enjoys sport (say which one and why).   _____

Theme : Co-operation 3 – Group Decisions

Warm Up Game – Find the Pair

Give each person a card which has a picture on it (these can be drawn or cut out of magazines). Each picture is one of a pair of things that go together e.g. a needle and a reel of cotton; a dustpan and a brush; a button and a buttonhole, and so on. The object of the game is to find your partner, without talking, and then sit down next to them.

A Round

A time when I co-operated with someone was ... and I felt ...

Activity

Making a group decision that is fair to everybody is often difficult, but this activity is one solution that invites everyone to participate and have the opportunity to state their case and try to persuade others to share their point of view.

Ask pupils to look in magazines and cut out articles, or have some ready, relating to topics they would like the class to discuss e.g. a picture of elephants might denote discussion of the ivory trade, or a cigarette advertisement might lead to a discussion about the pros and cons of smoking and related health matters. The pictures are then placed on the floor in the middle of the circle. Each person is given four adhesive circles of the same colour. (Pieces of gummed paper cut up are just as effective).

They then select the four topics they would like the class to discuss and place their stickers on them. Next, pupils work in pairs and repeat the exercise, this time with four circles between them and a different colour from the first round. This means that pupils have to work together to reach a decision. When they have stuck these down pupils are asked to work in groups of four with again only four stickers between them (a different colour again). They have to argue their case for including their choice before sticking them on the appropriate picture. The votes (circles on each picture) are then counted and the winner is the subject chosen to be debated.

Conference

- How did it feel if others in your group did not initially share your choice?
- Did you feel your point of view was listened to?
- Do you feel the final choice was democratic?

Concluding Game – Pile Up

One person tells everyone in the circle to move one place to the left if they answer the description e.g. he or she has an M in their name, they are wearing blue socks, they like marmalade.

Each time someone moves and finds the seat already occupied, they have to sit on that person's lap. After the next question, if either of them answers 'Yes' to the question, then they both have to move.

The game continues until there are two big 'pile ups' chasing each other round the circle, or until no-one can stand the strain any longer.

Theme : Co-operation 4 – Prisoners' Dilemma Game

Warm Up Game – I'm Counting On You

Cut a strip of card into three squares and write a number on each square. The three numbers are to add up to 100 (make this 20 for younger children).

For example:

20	5	10
30	75	50
50	20	40

Mix up the numbers and give one number to each person. Ask the pupils to go round the circle and find the other two numbers that will go with theirs to add up to 100. When they have found them they sit down together.

A Round

'Our group works best when we ...'

Activity

Two suspects are taken into custody and separated. The District Attorney is certain that they are guilty of a specific crime, but he does not have adequate evidence to convict them at a trial. He points out to each prisoner that he has two alternatives: to confess to the crime the police are sure they have done, or not to confess. If they both do not confess, then the District Attorney states he will book them on some very minor trumped up charge such as petty larceny and illegal possession of a weapon, and they would both receive minor punishments: if they both confess they will be prosecuted, but he will recommend less than the most severe sentence; but if one confesses and the other one does not, then the confessor will receive lenient treatment for turning state's evidence, whereas the latter will get 'the book' slapped at him. (Luce and Raiffa, 1957)

Read the *Prisoners' Dilemma* to the class. This game presents a dilemma in that one group will not know what the group playing opposite has chosen to do until the first group has also made its move. There is an element of guess work, trust and eventually co-operation involved if the groups are to succeed in their aim.

- Divide class into four groups – two groups playing opposite each other.
- Give each group a set of instructions and score sheets.
- Start the game. Teacher will act as intermediary between the groups.
- Encourage full participation, discussion and methods of arriving at a group decision.
- Complete all ten rounds.

Conference

- Was your group successful? If 'yes,' why? If 'no,' what stopped it succeeding?
- Did you feel you were listened to?
- Did your group co-operate: a) with one another: b) with the other group?
- Did communicating with the other group help?
- Can you think of any genuine situations where this game is played out for real?

Concluding Game – Tropical Storm

The whole class works together to make the sound of a storm in a rain forest. One person starts by rubbing his or her hands together. This is copied by the person on the left and so on round the circle until it reaches the first person. The action is then changed to snapping fingers and it gradually ripples round the circle. Remember to copy the actions of the person on your right and not the person who starts! Each time the action gets louder e.g slapping thighs, stamping feet to simulate the storm. As with any sudden shower, the volume decreases and this is done by reversing the actions until everyone holds out their palms to face the circle in silence as the rain storm ends and peace descends.

The Prisoners' Dilemma Game
Guidelines for Participants

Aim

The aim of the exercise is for your group to end up with a positive score.

The Game

You will be playing against another group.

Your group will be asked to decide whether to play **RED** or **BLUE.**

Write your answer in the space provided.

When both groups have decided you will be told what the other group played.

The Scores

If your group plays	and the other group plays	Your score	Their score
red	red	+ 3	+ 3
red	blue	- 6	+ 6
blue	red	+ 6	- 6
blue	blue	- 3	- 3

Instructions

1. There will be ten rounds.

2. After the 4th round, your group will be asked whether or not they want to confer.

3. The conference will only take place if BOTH groups make the request.

4. After the 8th round both groups WILL confer.

5. Scores in the 9th and 10th rounds may be doubled.

Round 1 ....   Round 6 ....

Round 2 ....   Round 7 ....

Round 3 ....   Round 8 ....

Round 4 ....   Round 9 ....

Round 5 ....   Round 10 ....

Adapted from the most famous experimental model for the study of co-operation.

Luce, R.D. and Raiffa, H. (1957) Games and Decisions New York: Wiley.

Mollie Curry and Carolyn Bromfield, 1994
NASEN Enterprises Ltd.

Gender

Even in an era when most schools are co-educational, it is interesting to note how children very quickly divide into separate gender groups and from these build up stereotype images of the sexes. Given a free choice of seating arrangements in Circle-time, it will be apparent to the teacher how divided his or her class are. We have frequently noticed the arc of boys on one side and girls on the other!

These activities are designed to explore some to the myths surrounding the gender issue and examine their own and others perceptions and attitudes towards the subject.

As with all Circle-times, mutual support and awareness is raised and this theme particularly enables relationships between boys and girls to remain easy and comfortable. Fostering true friendship and understanding, regardless of gender, is an enriching experience that helps to break down barriers and keep them down.

Through these sessions it may be revealed that males and females do have different ways of showing their feelings. So often, boys are bound by cultural expectations to hide their feelings except in the case of anger or aggression which is sometimes seen as 'acceptable in a boy'.

Circle-time will enable these issues to be addressed, and the discussions that are triggered can have productive outcomes if handled sensitively.

Encouraging boys and girls to work easily together has positive repercussions in the classroom.

Theme : Gender 1 – Occupations

Warm Up Game – Wink Swap

Divide the class into pairs – one boy and one girl. The boys sit on a chair and the girls stand behind. One girl stands behind an empty chair. All those standing should have their hands behind their backs. The object of the game is for the girl without a partner to find one by winking at one of the boys. The boys must stay alert and keep looking at the girl who is choosing a partner. When they are winked at, they must try to leave their seats and move to the space. The girls must be ready to put their hands gently on their partners shoulders to stop them from moving if they think their partners have been winked at. This game requires concentration and is good for practising looking at the person who is talking or in this case winking! After some successful attempts swap over and let the girls sit down.

A Round

'When I grow up I want to be ...'

Activity

Work in boy/girl pairs or groups of 4 (2 boys and 2 girls). Choose a scribe and discuss and write down jobs and occupations that are carried out by: a) women only b) men only c) both men and women.

Occupations

Women Only	Both Men and Women	Men Only

Conference

Each pair or group elects a spokesperson and reports back to whole class. Information is collated on a large sheet of paper.

When this is completed the teacher will get a picture of how the pupils view this aspect of the gender issue and how much work needs to be done to dispel the stereotypes e.g. only men can drive trucks, only women can be nurses etc. Get the class to question each item as it is read out and extract information that reinforces the idea that the majority of jobs can be done by both sexes. Collect books and pictures on the subject to share with the class.

Task

Ask the pupils to go home and compile a list of jobs round the home that:

a) are only done by the women and girls in the house;
b) are only done by the men and boys in the house;
c) are shared or done by both sexes.

Concluding Game – There's a space on my right

(Instructions on page 47) Play the game but add an extra rule that a boy must chose a girl and a girl must chose a boy.

Theme : Gender 2 – Boys And Girls

Warm Up Game – Throw a Name

Stand in a circle. Take a soft ball and throw it to someone of the opposite sex and say their name. The person who catches the ball has to throw it to someone else (boy to girl and girl to boy), and say their name until everybody has had a turn.

A Round

Girls are really good at ...   Boys are really good at ...

Activity

Divide class into mixed gender groups and give each group a sheet of paper folded in half. Each group will have different headings to describe their responses to different emotions e.g.

When girls are sad they ...	When boys are sad they ...

Other headings might be: a. When boys are angry they ... When girls are angry they ...

b. When girls are happy they ... When boys are happy they ...

c. When boys are upset they ... When girls are upset they ...

d. When girls are frightened they ... When boys are frightened they ...

Each group can appoint a scribe and a spokesperson. Make sure each person gets a chance to speak and is listened to.

Conference

Go round each group and elicit information which is then written on to a large sheet of paper headed: *How Do Boys and Girls Show Their Feelings?*

When the list is compiled, look down the responses and discuss with the class the similarities and the differences and which they think are effective and which are not. The effective responses could then be collated to form a resource book of effective strategies for dealing with emotions. Hopefully both sexes will be able to learn from one another.

Concluding Game – Word Associations

Everybody sits in a circle – boy girl, boy girl. The class claps out a rhythm e.g. knees; hands; knees hands, and then one person says a word such as 'Friend.' The whole class repeat the rhythm clap and the next person says a word associated with that word for example 'Play.' The next word might be 'Ball.' This continues until everybody in the circle has said a word.

How far removed from the beginning word was the word at the end?

Theme : Gender   3 – Using Stories

Warm Up Game – Spot the Difference

Pupils are seated boy-girl, boy-girl. One person is chosen to go outside the room. Whilst that person is outside, two pupils of the same sex swap places. The person outside has to come back in and guess who has moved. This will be an opportunity to practise skills of observation and memory.

A Round

I wish boys would ...   I wish girls would ...

Activity

Tell the story of Sleeping Beauty. Focus on the main characters: a beautiful princess; a wicked stepmother; a handsome prince.

Discuss some of their attributes, and characteristics. Ask the class for a list of their favourite fairy stories. Divide the class into mixed gender groups and give each group a fairy story to analyse using the 'Fairy Stories' worksheet – one per group. Each group is to appoint a scribe and a spokesperson.

Conference

Elicit information from each group. Are there any similarities?

• Are all the 'good' people beautiful and are all the 'bad' people ugly or wicked?

• Do all the stories have happy endings and is this like real life?

• Do you think that fairy stories help or hinder forming opinions about gender issues?

Concluding Game – Jack and Jill

A boy and a girl are in the middle of the circle. 'Jill' is blindfolded and tries to catch 'Jack' by calling out, 'Where are you Jack?' He replies, 'Here I am Jill.' She has one minute to catch him, both of them keeping within the circle. Those sitting down will gently guide the blindfolded person back into the centre if he or she comes towards the edge. After one minute, or less if Jack is caught, another couple is chosen with the boy being blindfolded this time.

Fairy Stories

The fairy story our group has chosen is _____

	Name	**Characteristics**
Main female character		
Main male character		
Good characters		
Bad characters		
How does the story end?		
Who wins?		
Who loses?		
Who is the hero/heroine?		

What is your favourite fairy story? _____

Think of other fairy stories.

Do the male and female characters always have the same attributes?

Mollie Curry and Carolyn Bromfield, 1994
NASEN Enterprises Ltd.

Theme : Gender 4 – Group Story Writing

Warm Up Game – Mickey Mouse

Everybody is given a piece of paper and they write down the name of a character, a film star, sports personality, or someone else they would like to be. On the back of the paper they write their names. All the pieces are then given to one person who is the keeper of the secrets. To begin with, the keeper reads out or writes on a large sheet of paper all the personalities. Then, going round the circle, everybody has a chance to guess who is who. If a character is guessed then the name is crossed off the list. This can continue going round the circle until everyone's identity is guessed.

A Round

'I chose my personality or character because ...'

Activity

Read a story where the gender characteristics are not stereotypes, for example *The Paper Bag Princess* by R. Munsch (published by Hippo Books).

Divide class into mixed gender groups.

Task.

Write a group story where the main characters have atypical characteristics e.g.
• the witch is good and the princess is evil
• the princess rescues the prince, and so on.

Make sure that each group is aware of how it should function so that all its members ideas are included. This could mean that there is one scribe who starts is the story off with one sentence. Each person can then contribute a sentence going round the group - several times if necessary - until the story is finished. Remind the group of rules such as :

1. Only one person talks at a time.
2. Everybody else looks at the person who is talking.
3. Everybody's ideas are valued.

Conference

When the stories are finished each group nominates a reader and then that person reads the story to the whole class. At a later stage these stories may be made into books and illustrated.

Ask for feedback on each story.
- Did they enjoy the task ?
- Did they feel they were listened to ?
- Did anybody in the group contradict an idea for example say 'a girl (a boy) wouldn't (or couldn't) do that' ?
- Do they prefer the class stories or the original fairy stories ?

Concluding Game - How do you do ?

The class sit on the floor - boy girl, boy girl. Two children get up (1 boy, 1 girl) and the circle closes to leave one space. They shake hands three times saying 'How do you do ?' each time. Once the greeting is complete they dash round the circle in opposite directions to see who can be first to sit in the vacant space. The person who is left chooses two new people to play the game and then takes one of their places.

Changes

Learning to cope with change is an important part of growing up. We all find it difficult at times and it is both useful and helpful to examine and explore this issue. Although this theme can be incorporated at any time during the school year it is most appropriate at the beginning and/or at the end of term. This helps pupils to anticipate and to look forward to as well as having the opportunity to reflect and look back.

The beginning of the year, or whenever the group is meeting together for the first time, presents an important opportunity for getting to know one another. Ensure the environment is safe and comfortable so that feelings can be explored and risks can be taken. This is important if any sign of distress is revealed during discussions.

Circle-time can be used to help children find out more about each other and for the teacher to glean insight into what makes the individuals 'tick'.

Most children these days have to cope with a whole variety of change situations. Exploring strategies, pooling ideas and feelings does help, and enables some of the subsequent feelings to be shared.

The *Changes* theme also gives children the chance to show that they are concerned, and that they do feel sympathetic to another's expressed need. It is a comfort to know that others have felt the same or similar emotions in response to events and that is 'O.K.' Most important of all, children learn that there aren't right or wrong feelings and that individuals can react in different ways.

Theme : Changes 1 – Time Line

Warm Up Game – Pass the Object

One person starts by holding an invisible object which they mime. The person next to them has to guess the object and then change it to something different. The new object is carefully mimed and then passed on to the next person. This is not a test and other people can help with the guesses.

A Round

'I am looking forward to ...'

Activity

Give each person a sheet of paper and ask them to draw a horizontal line (it need not be straight), across the paper. Now ask the children to mark the important or special dates in their life across the line. Children can write or draw the events and do not need to know the exact dates but only which events occurred before another. These might include: date of birth; starting school; moving house; birth of a sibling; a relative dying; learning a new skill; a celebration; passing an exam. The last entry on the line will be today in the current class or school.

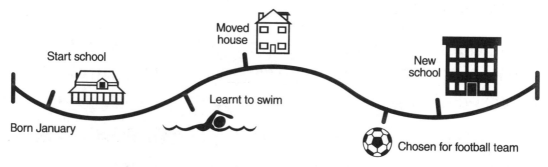

Conference

Invite children to share their time lines and give explanations as to their choice of events. Some children would be happier sharing with a friend and some may want the information to remain private:

• What were the good times and how did you feel?

• What were the bad times and how did you feel?

• Did you learn something about another person that you didn't know?

• Did anybody have the same experiences as you?

• This is an opportunity to 'join' together pupils and to make connections for them.

Concluding Games – Frog Hops

One person is the frog and sits in the middle of the circle on a piece of newspaper which represents the lily pad. The children then chant together:

'Hey, frog face, can we have some of your space?' The frog replies, 'Yes' and then puts in a condition such as 'Yes, but only if you have white socks.' All those who have white socks can then take one hop forward. This continues with a different condition each time and ends when someone has touched the frog on the shoulder. That person then becomes the frog and the game starts again.

Theme : Changes 2 – Reflecting on Changes

Warm Up Game – Class Web

One person starts with a large ball of wool and wraps it round his or her waist. The ball of wool is then passed to someone else in the circle who also wraps it around the waist. This continues, until everybody is in the web. The web can be untangled by passing the wool in reverse order. Rules can be introduced to this game, such as, 'Pass the wool to someone who you would like to change places with – and say why.'

A Round

'If I were an adult I would change ...'

Activity

The teacher needs to collect a set of newspaper and magazine articles or pictures that describe or show some change in people's circumstances. These could include wars and famines and events on a global scale, or things closer to home, such as the birth of a new baby or a new neighbour in the street.

Working in twos or threes, each is group is given up to four items and each person has to choose one. Each person shares his or her choice with the group and opens up a discussion on the issues and the feelings engendered. Finally, the group has to select one item to share with the whole group.

Conference

Ensure that one spokesperson is chosen for each group and that each has only one item. That person reflects the reason for his or her choice and the feelings it generated.

The whole group can then discuss what they think could be done to help the people cope with their changes. Identify common threads and join together groups with similar ideas, then thank each group for their contribution.

Concluding Game – Statues

Each child is given a bean bag which he or she balances on his or her head. The children then move around the circle to some music. If someone drops their beanbag, they have to change into a statue and stand still. They can move again when someone picks up the beanbag and replaces it. This game is fun and encourages co-operation and a caring attitude.

Theme : Changes 3 – Welcome

Warm Up Game – Who's Got the Warm Fuzzy?

Make a woolly pompom. Someone sits in the middle of the circle and closes his or her eyes. Everybody else then passes the Warm Fuzzy round from hand-to-hand (you can pass more than one if you have a large group). When they are doing this they say, 'Round and round the Warm Fuzzy goes. Where it stops nobody knows.' At that point, everybody puts their hands behind their backs. The person in the middle opens his or her eyes and tries to guess who has the Warm Fuzzy.

A Round

When I was new in this school I felt ...

Activity

Being new to a school can be quite a daunting experience (ask any supply teacher!) Why not make a 'Welcome Book,' with information about the class and the school to show to anybody who joins the school during the year? Divide the class into groups and allocate the tasks: the front cover; introduction; plan of the building; timetable; school/class rules; rewards/privileges; out of school activities; uniform; playtime activities; staff list.

Each pupil could write a brief autobiography. Photographs of pupils and school events could also be included.

Conference

Each group should be given an opportunity to share the information before the book is assembled.

- Will the book be useful?
- Is there anything else we should include?
- What else can we do to welcome someone who is new?

Concluding Game – Change Places

Everybody in the circle is on their hands and knees. Number the pupils alternately 1 and 2. When your number is called out you move one limb forward. The idea is to get to the other side of the circle. The centre of the circle can become very congested and a great deal of co-operation is needed for the whole class to be successful.

Theme : Changes 4 – Saying Goodbye

Warm Up Game – When I Leave This Class

The first person begins by saying 'When I leave this class I will take ...' (they name something in the class e.g. a desk). The second person says, 'When I leave this class, I will take a desk and a ...'(adding another item). This continues round the circle with everybody helping if necessary.

A Round

When I first came to this class I remember ...

It might be appropriate to mention that it is OK to have good and bad memories and to discuss those which they would like to forget and those they would like to keep.

Activity

Saying goodbye at the end of a school year is often difficult and painful. This activity is fun and allows everybody to be affirmed by their friends. It also leaves them with a memento to take with them to remind them of all the happy times they have shared together throughout the year.

Give everybody (even the teacher) a piece of card with a loop of string attached. They each put the card over their head and let it hang down their back. The whole class is then invited to write on everybody's card some positive message saying: why you like that person; what you will remember about them, or what they are good at. This is very similar to *Special Person*, but because you are relying on the children to make sure their comments are positive, it is best done with a class you have worked with for some time.

This is a fun activity, as very often long conga lines appear round the classroom as people are all writing on one another's backs – its worth having the camera ready! Do not allow anyone to read their paper backs until they are all complete. When everyone is finished, the children take them off, sit down and read them.

Conference

Ask children to contribute a selection of favourite comments:

• What did they feel about not being able to see what was being written?

• How did they feel when they read their cards?

Concluding Game – 'It's been good to know you'

One person stands in the middle of the circle with his or her eyes closed, and someone is chosen to say 'It's been good to know you' in a disguised voice. The person in the middle then has to try and guess who said it. When the identity has been guessed, some one else is chosen to go in the middle.

Conflict Resolution

Conflicts are an inevitable part of school life due to people having different opinions, interests and goals. It is therefore useful to identify areas of conflict with a view to reducing or minimising their cause. Conflict need not be a negative situation if we learn and grow from its outcome.

So many times children repeat the same ineffectual solution to a problem which leads to rejection or confrontation. Children's skills in dealing with, and avoiding, conflict varies enormously and teachers are in a central position to develop and teach children a wide range of strategies enabling them to have a real choice about their behaviour. Dealing with conflict in a positive way enables those children who are socially skilled to become models and a resource for others.

Circle-time gives children the time and space to consider their own or other people's actions that may have contributed to the conflict and allows them to do so in a calm environment. Children can learn to ask for help from their peers and their teacher and together they can work towards finding solutions. As each class builds up its own repertoire of strategies, so individual repertoires widen and act as a preventative measure. Together the class can work through its problems and work towards forming a more cohesive group.

The children begin to see how much they have in common with one another instead of just seeing their differences. The spirit of competition becomes replaced by an atmosphere of empathy and mutual assistance. This co-operative process is more effective in changing behaviour than individual instruction as it relies on group adherence – that sense of wanting to belong.

Circle-time gives children the time and space to consider their own or other people's actions that may have contributed to a conflict. It affords the opportunity to assess the antecedents and consequences of any behaviour and for children to make the connection between their behaviour and the effect it has on others. Self-discipline and development of an inner code of responsibility is encouraged.

Theme : Conflict Resolution 1 – Active Listening

Warm-up Game – Clapping Game

One person goes outside the room. The rest of the group decides on an object for the person to find. The person outside is then invited back in and he or she has to guess the object whilst the group claps. The closer to the object that the person gets so the louder the group claps. When they are far away the clapping is very soft.

A Round

I wish grown ups would listen when I ...

Activity

For any conflict to be satisfactorily resolved, both parties need to **listen** to the needs of each other. This is a skill which needs to be practised and the following activities will allow children to practise these skills before going on to tackle any conflict resolution exercises.

Work with a partner. Pairs call themselves A and B. A's will talk and B's will listen. These exercises can be repeated reversing the roles. Write the instructions on postcards and give them out so that partners cannot see.

Activity 1
A: Talk to your partner about what you do at home and at the weekends your hobbies, favourite T.V. programmes, and so on.
B: When your partner speaks, try to be as disinterested as possible. Look around the room and inspect the floor, fiddle with your watch, be as bored as possible. ***Do not make eye-contact.***

Activity 2
A: Continue talking about your hobbies interests, what you had for breakfast and so on.
B: This time keep interrupting. Try to take over the conversation, talking about your own free time.

Activity 3
A: Talk to your partner about your dream holiday – money no object, taking anybody of your choice etc.
B: This time ***pay attention!***

Look at the person, nod, sit slightly forward, make eye-contact, smile. Say things like: 'Oh yes! – mm – I see!' Give them your full undivided attention. You are now active listening. Be aware of people becoming uncomfortable during these exercises and stop at the appropriate moment.

Conference

Elicit and Record:
A: In Activity 1 and 2 how did you feel when you were talking to someone who was obviously not listening? Did you find it difficult to carry on? What did you do? What did you want to do?
B: In Activity 1 and 2 how did you feel having to ignore what was said?
How much information did you pick up even though you were trying not to listen?

Now think back to Activity 3.
A: How did you feel this time? In what way was it different?
B: How did you feel this time? How much information did you pick up?

Concluding Game - Whisper Sing Shout!

(see instructions on page 54)

Key Points to Being a Good Listener

FOCUS:
Give attention
Lean forward
Maintain eye-contact
Do not interrupt or offer opinion

ACCEPT:
Nod and smile
Show you understand
Give respect

EXTEND:
Ask questions such as:
Are you saying that ...?
How did you feel when ...?
It seems to me that ...
Could you say a bit more about ...?
What do you think about ...?

Mollie Curry and Carolyn Bromfield, 1994
NASEN Enterprises Ltd.

THIS PAGE MAY BE PHOTOCOPIED

Theme : Conflict Resolution 2 – Name Calling

Warm-up Game – Action Name Game

Stand in a circle. One person begins by choosing an action to mime which for example, starts with the same letter as his or her name, Hopping Holly and Walking William. As the person says the name, he or she begins to mime and when other people have guessed the action they join in. Continue round the circle until everybody has had a go.

A Round

'When people call me a friendly nickname I feel ...'
'When people tease me and call me names I do not like I feel ...'
(Record the feelings on a chart)

Some names are friendly and we feel ...	Some names are hurtful and we feel ...

Activity

Finding strategies for dealing with name calling:

Start by collecting information about some of the reasons that people are picked on or teased for ... Record these on a large sheet of paper (see example on page 113).

In pairs, talk about children's experiences of name-calling and teasing. Make sure children are in a pair in which they feel comfortable. Stress confidentiality. Some children may want to share these experiences with t whole group.

What shall we do about it? Use the ABC Action Plan to brainstorm some solutions.

ASK   – What can we do when people call us names?
BRAINSTORM   – Ways of dealing with it;
CHOOSE   – Choose some things to try.

These could then be recorded in a book, so that pupils could be reminded of some of the strategies they could try when faced with teasing.

Conference

It is helpful to establish a code of practice in dealing with name calling which could form part of a whole school policy. This should: a) help children deal with it; b) give strategies to try; c) decrease incidents; d) offer protection to those who are on the receiving end; e) give consequences of their behaviour to those who offend.

Evaluate the policy after a few days or a week. Rate the strategies according to those that seem effective. If pupils find new strategies they can be added to the list.

Concluding Game – Sausages

One person is in the middle of the circle. That person must try not to laugh. The people round the edge will take it in turns to ask questions, to which the middle person must always answer, 'Sausages.' For example 'What do you wash your hands with?' Answer – 'Sausages!'   If the middle person laughs then he or she changes places with someone and the game starts again.

We get picked on for the way we act and the way we look. We have been teased for ...

the clothes I wear

my odd socks

wearing glasses

my weight

my fringe

my lst name

my birthmark

my speech

my trainers

my haircut

my brace

my height

being small

being tall

Mollie Curry and Carolyn Bromfield, 1994
NASEN Enterprises Ltd.

The ABC of Problem Solving

Ask: 'What is the problem?' and LISTEN to the answers.

Brainstorm: 'What could we do to solve it?' Write down three ideas that you think are good

Choose: DISCUSS all the ideas until you AGREE what to do. The agreement:

Is it fair? _____

Is it sensible? _____

Will it work? _____

Mollie Curry and Carolyn Bromfield, 1994
NASEN Enterprises Ltd.

Theme : Conflict Resolution 3 – The Six Point Star Plan

Warm Up Game – Who Stole the Cookie from the Cookie Jar?

Number the players round the circle. Everybody starts to chant, 'Who stole the cookies from the cookie jar?' One person replies, 'Number 1 stole the cookies from the cookie jar.' Number 1 replies, 'Who me?' Whole class: 'Yes you!' Number 1 'Couldn't be!' Whole class: 'Then who?' Number 1 then chooses another number from the circle and says 'Number 12, or another number, stole the cookies from the cookie jar!' and the game continues. If someone fails to respond when their number is called, they could choose to do a forfeit!

A Round

'I am trying to be better at ...'

Activity

This can be in response to a situation that has recently occurred or pupils can offer conflicts that are still unresolved. This process can also be practised using a hypothetical situation where no personalities are involved and everybody can take a dispassionate view.

Conflict Situation

A group of children are playing with a ball during break. Another child wants to join the game but is refused entry to the game. The child waits and watches for a while and then sees two other children approaching who ask to join. The group lets these two join in the game. This upsets the first child and an argument starts.

Use the Six Point Problem Solving Plan to work out a solution that meets both sides needs. This activity can be done in groups or with the whole class and children can role play the different characters in the scene.

This conflict is taken from real life. When the original group explained that their need was to have an equal number on each team, and that was the reason they had refused entry to the first child, it became a much simpler conflict to resolve and made the whole issue less personal. All they had to do was explain their reasoning to the first child and he or she could then have gone away and found a partner to join the game. When tackled in this way, there are often very simple solutions to the problem and if children are taught to express their needs, it will often prevent a conflict from getting out of hand.

Conference

- Were both parties happy with the outcome?
- Did it meet everybody's needs?
- Did you get into a 'win-win' situation? (Use diagram to show how this is possible.)
- Do you think you could use this formula for solving other problems?

Concluding Game – Rainbow

Pupils sit in circle on chairs with a gap between each chair. In the centre of the circle are some keys. The pupils are named colours round the circle – red, yellow, green and blue. When the red group is called, they walk or hop clockwise round the outside of the circle and attempt to get in front of their own chair and pick up the keys. The player who picks up the keys gets to call the next colour, but they are not allowed to call their own group.

The teacher may call out, 'Rainbow.' The group which is walking round have to change direction and walk anti-clockwise to collect the keys. This ensures that it is not always the fastest walker or hopper that gets them!

The 6 Point Star Plan for Resolving Conflicts

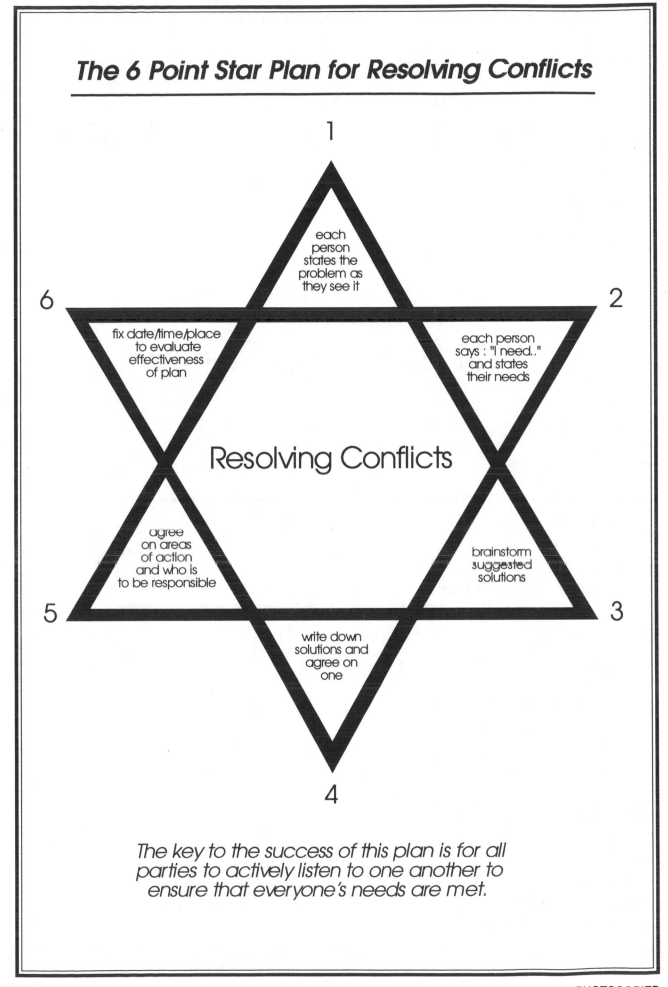

1

each person states the problem as they see it

6

fix date/time/place to evaluate effectiveness of plan

2

each person says : "I need.." and states their needs

Resolving Conflicts

5

agree on areas of action and who is to be responsible

3

brainstorm suggested solutions

4

write down solutions and agree on one

The key to the success of this plan is for all parties to actively listen to one another to ensure that everyone's needs are met.

Mollie Curry and Carolyn Bromfield, 1994
NASEN Enterprises Ltd.

Trying to Resolve a Conflict Using a Win-Win Solution.

The ideal solution to a conflict is one where there are no winners or losers and where both parties needs are met.

The Situation :

Tracey : "I want to play with the bricks and knock them over."

Shane : "I want to read my book and I can't concentrate."

	Tracey gets what she needs	*Tracey doesn't get what she needs*
Shane gets what he needs	**win-win**	**win-lose**
Shane doesn't get what he needs	**win-lose**	**lose-lose**

One solution to the conflict could be that one of them stops doing what he or she wants to do, but this compromise will not meet the needs of both of them.

Can you suggest a way of resolving this conflict that will lead to a win-win outcome ?

Mollie Curry and Carolyn Bromfield, 1994
NASEN Enterprises Ltd.

Theme : Conflict Resolution 4 – Reading the Signs

Warm Up Game – Skin the Snake

Pupils stand one behind the other with a break in the circle at one point. Each person puts his or her right hand through his or her own legs to take the left hand of the person behind. The pupil at the end of the line kneels down and crouches with his or her head well tucked in. Starting from the beginning of the break, the circle moves slowly backwards over the last person until the last but one person is at the back and is able to crouch down. This process continues until the entire circular line has moved back over itself and are all crouching on the floor.

A Round

'Arguments make me feel ...'

Activity

Divide the class into groups. Give each group a large sheet of paper with the word conflict in the middle. Ask them to make a 'word web' with as many different words that describe their feelings and thoughts during a conflict.

Next try to brainstorm, still within the group, as many strategies for coping with conflicts (fights, arguments, and so on) as possible. Write them down on another large piece of paper, for example:

Strategies

Count to 10;	Listen to the other person;	Keep cool;
Take more time;	Think clearly;	Stay calm;
Walk away;	Find a friend;	Respect their opinion;
Tell someone;	Introduce humour;	Compromise.

Conference

Share the feelings and strategies from the first two lists with the whole group. Next, discuss with the class one of the best strategies for conflict resolution – that is *avoiding* them! Ask the pupils what non-verbal, and verbal signs would indicate that a conflict might be imminent:

Non-verbal	Verbal
grinding teeth;	tone of voice;
going red in the face;	complaining;
frowning;	shouting;
scowling;	saying no;
sweaty palms;	sarcasm;
clenched fists;	laughing at you;
fidgeting;	loud voice;
going very quiet.	disagreeing with everything.

Pupils need to cue into these signs and become skilful at recognising them in themselves and in others.

Concluding Game - Co-operative letters

Pupils to work in two's or three's and to form letters of the alphabet. Larger groups could make up people's names or the whole group could try making a word like 'co-operation.'

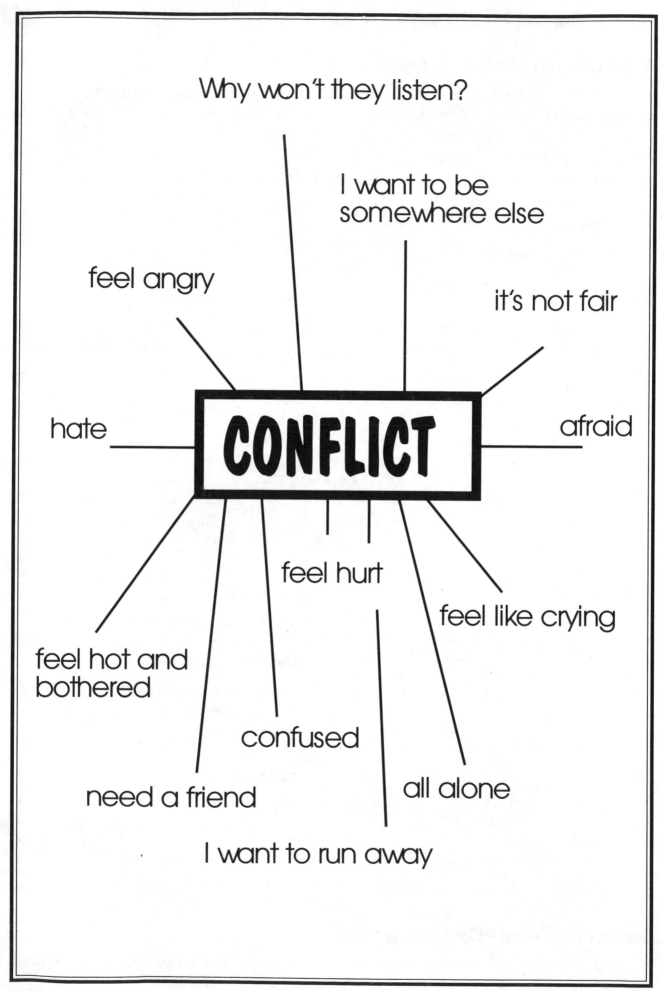

Why won't they listen?

I want to be somewhere else

feel angry

it's not fair

hate

CONFLICT

afraid

feel hurt

feel like crying

feel hot and bothered

confused

need a friend

all alone

I want to run away

Mollie Curry and Carolyn Bromfield, 1994
NASEN Enterprises Ltd.

Problem Solving

Circle-time is the ideal forum for discussing problems in a non-emotional environment and for discovering problem-solving methods that can be used to find creative solutions. Children can ask for help from their teacher and from their peers. The experiential learning that takes place in Circle-time is invaluable. Giving a child the opportunity to 'own' a problem helps to internalise the concept.

In Circle-time everyone benefits from social skills training, from being able to identify the best way to handle a situation and attain some goal. All of this can be valuable training in problem-solving for a group of children. Having your opinion listened to and evaluated can be self-affirming, also the assistance of others in evaluating a course of action that has been decided on.

An important aspect of identifying problems is the fact that it is done anonymously or in the third person. For example:

'A boy I know tripped me up when I was playing football,' or, 'I have seen some people fiddling with other peoples' bikes.'

This facilitates the discussion and, as no names are mentioned, one person cannot be victimised. The trust and 'safety' of the circle is maintained. (Of course, if teachers get to hear of serious misdemeanours they must be dealt with individually out of the circle). Being able to discuss problems reduces feelings of isolation, i.e. 'It's not only me that doesn't like going out to play, others feel like that too, and for similar reasons.' It enables pupils to see each other's problems and to give immediate support. It will also reduce a build up of resentment or anger that may smoulder or boil over into rage.

Problem Solving in Circle-time provides a forum for the problem, somewhere to 'lay it down' and then to receive strategies and ideas to solve it. It is the teacher's role to ensure that there is some evaluation and/or follow up to establish how effective the solutions have been. Teachers who can model constructive problem solving and who are interested in finding solutions will greatly enhance the chances of their pupils being successful.

Theme : Problem Solving 1 – Smiley Classroom

Warm Up Game – Pass the Smile

The first person takes the smile off his or her face and passes it to the next one, who is looking very solemn until the smile is given. They then smile and become radiant! The smile is passed all round the circle.

A Round

'Something that made me really happy this week was ...'

Activity

What makes a Smiley Classroom?

Divide the class into groups and ask them to think about their classroom, and about working together.

What makes it easy to work together and what makes it difficult?

What makes it a happy place to come to each day and what hinders this process?

Each group can choose a scribe and write the ideas on a chart:

What helps? ...	What hinders? ...

Conference

Each group brings back the information and shares it with the whole class.

Looking at the 'helps' and 'hinders' elicit positive things that the pupils could do to make their classroom a smiley place. Choose three or four to have as rules for the week or longer. This negotiation with the pupils is important as it makes them realise that rules are aimed at all members of the group. By taking part in the formulation of the rules for their class they will 'own' them and therefore be more likely to abide by them.

Guidelines for making rules

1. Rules should be positively phrased. Avoid a list of don'ts, as negative rules do not teach. It is more effective to teach a desirable behaviour than to eradicate an undesirable one.

2. Rules should be written in observable terms. For rules to be effective they need to be refer to behaviours that are clearly apparent and therefore able to be reinforced frequently.

3. Rules should be clearly displayed for easy reference. Younger children may need colour coding or symbols to assist communication.

4. Be flexible and open to change. Rules can change as the needs of the class change.

Concluding Game - All Tangled Up

Two people leave the room. All the remaining people join hands except two so that there is a beginning and an end. Everybody twists and turns themselves into a lovely tangle without letting go of hands. The two people are then invited back to untangle the class.

How to Make a Smiley Classroom

ASK:
What makes a smiley classroom?

BRAINSTORM:
What can we do to make this a happy place?

CHOOSE:
Choose 3 or 4 ideas to try this week.

_____

_____

_____

Mollie Curry and Carolyn Bromfield, 1994
NASEN Enterprises Ltd.

Theme : Problem Solving 2 – The Playground

Warm Up Game – Call a Name

One person stands in the centre of the circle with a ball. He or she bounce the ball as high as they can and calls out someone's name. That person has to run into the circle and catch the ball before it bounces again. Continue until everybody has had a go.

A Round

'In the playground I feel ...'

Activity

An area of concern for many children and teachers is conflicts which arise daily in the playground, and for which there seems to be no creative solutions. Some of the problems stem from children being bored due to the lack of a stimulating environment. This Circle-time could provide the starting point for minor changes in the playground which could then develop into a whole school project, resulting in major changes in organisation.

In groups, complete the chart about what pupils like and dislike about playtime. This will give you initial information about some of the problems.

Things I like about playtime	Things I don't like about playtime

In twos or threes write down, sketch or plan improvements or additions to the play area. This Circle-time could be developed as a cross-curricular theme involving, maths, language, science, technology, art etc. Changes in organisation and facilities can be included as well as designing equipment and play materials.

Conference

- Each group is to report back its ideas to the whole class.

- Encourage discussion about feasibility and practicalities.

- Record all suggestions and amendments.

- Design an action plan to include:

    a) what is to be done; b) how it is to be done; c) by whom.

Concluding Game – Duck, Duck, Goose

One person walks round the outside of the circle and touches people on the head saying, 'Duck' each time. When they are ready they touch someone's head and this time they say 'Goose.' The person who is the 'goose' gets up and runs after that person who in turn has to run round the circle and try to get back to the empty space. The person who is left standing starts the process again by touching heads and saying, 'Duck.' Try to make sure everybody is involved in the game and that children understand they are not to say 'goose' to someone who has already run. Perhaps the class could devise a signal as a reminder?

 # Things I like about playtime ...

 # Things I don't like about playtime ...

Theme : Problem Solving 3 – The Four Point Star Plan

Warm Up Game – Dracula

One person is chosen who is Dracula. He or she must walk slowly across the circle in 'robotic' mode, and try to touch the shoulder of a designated person. To stop Dracula from attacking them, they must call out the name of another person in the circle (not someone sitting next to them). If they fail to name another person, by the time they are touched on the shoulder, then they swap places and become Dracula.

A Round

'The biggest problem for me at school is ...'

Activity

As has been discussed in the previous Circle-time, many of the problems that children face occur in the playground, often due to lack of stimulation or not enough adult supervision, or lack of any rules. Too often valuable teaching time is taken up by the teacher listening to both sides of an argument and then acting as adjudicator, or arbitrator (we've all done it!). Children can be given the skills to settle an argument or disagreement *without* the intervention of an adult, and Circle-time can be used to practise these skills, employing role play situations. Sometimes, it is useful to provide an intermediary and another child could be invited to join the adversaries to assist in finding a solution to the problem. The teacher does not necessarily expect to hear the settlement but the pupils are expected to return to the room and be able to act in a civil manner towards each other.

Another process that can be used for third party facilitation when resolving a conflict is to use the 'Four Stages of Problem Solving.' Take a perennial problem like use of the playground for ball games. The boys want to play football: the girls want to play netball. Get both parties to go through the four sections and answer the questions:
- What happened?
- How do you feel about it?
- What would you like to happen?
- What could you actually do about it?

This process can be use for resolving conflicts between two people or between larger groups.

Conference

- Did the parties involved manage to come up with a solution to suit both of their needs?
- Do they think it will work?
- Do they think that this is a good way of solving problems?
- Do they think it necessary to make a written agreement?
- How long would they be prepared to give a solution to see if it works?

Concluding Game – Trains

One person pretends to be a train and 'chugs' up to another person in the circle and says, 'Hi! I'm Mike, who are you?' They reply, 'I'm Chris' (or whatever their name is). The first person says, 'Hurrah! Join my train.' The second person holds the first one round the waist and together they chug off to another person. The first one says, 'Hi! I'm Mike' The second one says, 'I'm Chris' and the first one says 'Who are you?' This process is repeated until everyone is in one long train. If you have a large class you may want to start more than one train.

The 4 Point Star Plan for Problem Solving

This process can be used as third party facilitation for resolving a conflict.

1 Each person has a turn to say what happened. The 'mediator' checks back for accuracy.

2 Each person has a turn to say how they feel about events. Record problem and feelings.

3 Each person has a turn to say what they would like to happen to solve the problem.

4 The mediator helps both parties to reach agreement on a solution that is fair and is likely to be successful.

By using a third child two arguing children can be helped to look at the difficulties and resolve them.
At first the teacher will need to model this process, but with practise children can begin to use this plan on their own.

Mollie Curry and Carolyn Bromfield, 1994
NASEN Enterprises Ltd.

Theme : Problem Solving 4 – Saying Something Difficult

Warm Up Game – Fruit Salad

Choose four fruits and go round the circle giving each person the name of one of the fruits. When a fruit is called out, all the people who have been given that particular fruit have to get up and find a new place. If you feel brave, call out 'Fruit salad!'   and then everybody has to change places!

A Round

'I find it difficult to ...'

Activity

Give out the 'Problems Page' worksheet and ask pupils to complete it. This task can be done individually, in pairs, or groups. Children could also look at the 'Difficult Situations' sheet and use these for group discussions. They can then decide what they would do and say on each of the occasions.

Conference

Children and adults need to learn how to communicate their feelings and give someone they are in dispute with, information about their behaviour and the effect it has on others.

Using '**I Statements,**' which are not an attack on the person but on their behaviour will protect self-esteem and reduce conflict.

'I statements have three components:

The behaviour – pushing John over.

The effect – John cut his knee.

The feelings – he feels very upset.

A good way to start an 'I' message is to begin with:

When you (label the behaviour), it (give information about the effect), and I feel (name the feelings)

For example: When you interrupt by talking during story time, it disturbs people around you so that they can't listen and I feel irritated.

Another important way of communicating feelings is to teach children to say:

'I like you, but I don't like it when you ... (name the behaviour).'

This is very simple but very powerful and extremely effective.

Concluding Game – No You Didn't

The group chooses a leader. The leader says, 'When I went to the Himalayas I found a ... (any object).' While saying this, the leader has to include some vocal or bodily action that the rest of the group have to spot. It could be arms folded, or a nod of the head, or a slight cough. Each person in the circle has to repeat the sentence and say an object, but try to include the action if they have spotted it. If they get it right the leader will say, 'Yes, you went to the Himalayas.' If they didn't get it right, the leader says, 'No, you didn't!'

Problems Page

1. **If someone called me a name I would feel (draw your face)**
   Then I would:
   a) tell the teacher.
   b) call them a name back.
   c) laugh at the joke as if I didn't care.
   d) ignore them.

2. **If there was a fight going on in the playground I would feel**
   Then I would:
   a) Walk away and have nothing to do with it.
   b) Join in the fight.
   c) Try to stop the fight.
   d) Tell the teacher.

3. **If I was blamed for something I didn't do I would feel**
   Then I would:
   a) Say 'That's not fair!' and walk away.
   b) Take the blame.
   c) Shout at the person who was blaming me.
   d) Try to stay calm and talk to the person.

4. **If someone was being nasty to my friend I would feel**
   Then I would:
   a) Tell my friend to ignore them.
   b) Be nasty back to that person.
   c) Gang up on the person.
   d) Be extra nice to my friend.

5. **If I was bullied at school I would feel**
   Then I would:
   a) Stay away from school.
   b) Bully someone smaller than myself.
   c) Tell someone.
   d) Keep the secret to myself.

Mollie Curry and Carolyn Bromfield, 1994
NASEN Enterprises Ltd.

DIFFICULT SITUATIONS

What can I say?

1. Someone who lives near you, who your Mum likes you to be friends with, keeps picking on you but Mum won't listen and says you're being silly.
You decide to tell your friend how you feel, but don't want to offend them.
What can you say?

2. Every time you go out to play the same child takes your ball and runs off with it. You and your friends are really angry but are nervous of saying anything because the child is older and is sometimes a bully. **What can you say?**

3. Someone in your class keeps borrowing your rubber and sharpener and whenever you want them you have to go and ask for them back. You are beginning to be fed up with this.
What can you say?

4. Every time you and your best friend want a private chat another child interrupts. You want to be friends with them, but don't want them around all the time.
What can you say?

5. A new child in your class calls you names. You don't want to be unkind as he's new.
What can you say?

Mollie Curry and Carolyn Bromfield, 1994
NASEN Enterprises Ltd.

Nursery and Reception Class

The following Circle-time plans are appropriate for nursery and reception classes as they illustrate a suitable length and framework for this age group. It is important to be sensitive to the need for a shorter, 'snappier' Circle-time, focusing on one succinct point so as not to elongate it beyond their concentration span and interest level.

When the teacher feels confident about using Circle-time, he or she can modify any of the circle plans to suit the needs of the class. All of the themes in this book have been adapted and used successfully with reception class children.

When initially starting Circle-time, set the ground rules so that the children understand the framework and know where the boundaries are. This will ensure that everybody has fun and that nobody can spoil anyone else's fun! With young children three rules are sufficient and these could be:

1. Only one person speaks at a time.

2. Listen to the person who is speaking.

3. Have fun and don't spoil anybody else's fun !

These Circle-times aim to focus on listening and talking to one another, taking turns and enjoying co-operative games ... sharing fun together.

Theme : Reception Class 1 – Smiles

Warm Up Game – Pass the Smile

Each child starts with a very sad face. The first child passes a hand over his or her face and, and in doing so, a smile appears as if by magic. They then pretend to take the smile and pass it to the person next to them who takes the smile and washes it onto their face. This continues until the whole class is smiling.

A Round

Something that makes me smile is ...

Activity

All the children are to walk round the circle and greet everybody in the class with a smile and say, 'Hello ... (say the person's name).' Wait until the person you are greeting greets you back before walking on to find the next one.

Have a smile competition where each child, going round in the circle, has to smile in a certain fashion and if they do they receive a badge to wear. (Each child **will** be successful!)

For example:
- smile prettily
- give a long smile
- give a toothy grin
- smile in a shy way

- smile sweetly
- smile cheekily
- give a silly smile
- smile in a friendly way

Conference

Discuss how they feel when they are smiling.

What did they notice happened when they smiled at somebody? The teacher could discuss how interactions between people are very often a mirror of the first behaviour e.g. If somebody smiles at you, you smile back.

If someone says something nasty to you the temptation is to respond by being horrible back to them.

If we try to be pleasant and polite and kind to people it is likely that they will be nice to us. Let's try and have a nice smiley classroom all day – (week, year!)

Concluding Game – Smile Swap

One child smiles at someone across the circle. When the smile is returned, they swap places. Someone else is chosen to smile and this continues until all the children have moved.

Mollie Curry and Carolyn Bromfield, 1994
NASEN Enterprises Ltd.

Theme : Reception Class 2 – Join Us

Warm Up Game – All Change

The teacher calls out an attribute and all the children to whom it applies have to get up and find another seat. For example : All the children who have black shoes.

All the children who like chocolate.

All the children who have a pet.

A Round

'If I had one wish it would be ...'

Activity

Get children to stand in the middle of the circle. The teacher will then call out two objects, places etc. and tell the children which side of the circle represents each one. The children then make a choice and go to appropriate side. For example: bluebells or buttercups.

When the children are in the two groups they turn to someone who has made the same choice as them and tell them why they made that choice, for example: 'My favourite colour is blue so I chose bluebells.' Examples of other choices could be:

sausages or beefburgers	rabbits or guinea pigs
roller boots or skate boards	honey or jam
indoors or outdoors	snow or sunshine

Conference

This Circle-time enables children to be 'joined' together and made aware of how many things they have in common with other people. Sometimes they are surprised, especially when it's with children they don't normally play with. This activity can help reduce isolation and encourage new friendships – 'Oh ! I didn't know you liked _____too.'

During the conference time the teacher acts as a facilitator to assist children with making the connections, for example 'If Nathan had one wish he wished people wouldn't hurt animals – and Abigail wished that too.'

Concluding Game – Magic Squeeze

Children hold hands and one person gently squeezes the hand of the person on his or her left or right. (they can choose). That person then passes the squeeze on to the person next to them until the squeeze has passed all round the circle. This is a magic squeeze and it only works if everybody is silent and concentrating very hard to make the magic work! A lovely, calm uniting way to end a Circle-time.

Theme : Reception Class 3 – Making Friends

Warm Up Game – Hello!

Each child has to turn to the person next to them and say, 'Hello' and then say their name, for example, 'Hello. I'm Alex.' This continues round the circle until everybody has introduced themselves.

A Round

'My best friend is ...'

Activity

Ask the children to turn to the person next to them and tell each other who they will play with today at breaktime or lunchtime and why they like playing with that person.

Conference

Discuss with the class what attributes (use simpler language) they would look for in a friend and how you can show people that you like them.

Teacher to write down on a large sheet of paper:

We can make friends by ...

He or she can then write down the answers which can be displayed on the wall or made into a book to remind children about the necessary skills needed for making friends.

An extension to this circle, would be to discuss with the children how we maintain friendships and the kinds of things friends do and don't do, for example, friends don't hurt each other etc.

Concluding Game – Pass the Hug

Pass a friendly hug around the circle.

Theme : Reception Class 4 – The Most Special Person

Warm Up Game – Hello Swap

One child gets up and walks across the circle and says, 'Hello' to another child and takes his or her place in the circle. That child then gets up and goes to say 'Hello' to someone else in the circle until every child has moved. They may need to devise a signal (such as arms folded) to show who has already been greeted. This ensures everyone is included and that nobody gets left out.

A Round

'The most special person to me is ...'

Activity

Pass round a box and tell the pupils that they are to lift the lid and look inside and there they will see the most special person in the world. Tell them not to show anybody else, but to just look, close the lid and pass the box on. The box will actually contain a mirror and so they will see themselves. Ask the children who have seen inside the box to keep the secret until everyone has had a look.

Conference

Who was the most special person? They should all say, 'Me!'
What did it feel like when you first looked inside?
What were you expecting?

Discuss with the class how it is possible for each of them to be the most special person, the qualities they each possess and about the uniqueness of individuals.

Concluding Game – The train song

Choose one child to be the train and get ten children to join on behind to be the trucks (they can hold on to the child's waist who is in front). All the class sing the song and the 'train' goes round the inside of the circle, dropping off one truck each time until there are none left. This is a useful fun activity for practising counting and can be played more than once so that everybody gets a go.

The train is carrying coal,
It has 10 trucks you'll find
At every station the train will stop,
And leave one truck behind.

References

Ballard, J (1982) *Circlebook,* Irvington: New York.

Bond, T (1986) *Games For Social Skills,* Hutchinson: London.

Borba, M and Borba, C (1978) *Self-Esteem:* A Classroom Affair Harper and Row: London.

Borba, M and Borba, C (1982) *Self-Esteem:* A Classroom Affair (Volume 2), Harper and Row: London.

Brandes, D and Phillips, H (1979) *Gamesters' Handbook,* Hutchinson: London.

Brandes, D (1982) *Gamesters' Handbook* Two, Hutchinson: London.

Bromfield, C (1992) *The Effectiveness of Circle-time as a Strategy for Use in Primary Schools with Special Regard to Children Having Behaviour Problems,* Unpublished M.Ed (SEN) Dissertation. University of Plymouth.

Burns, R B (1979) *The Self-Concept,* Longman: London.

Button, L (1976) *Outline Programme Developmental Groupwork Action Research Project,* School of Education, University of Exeter.

Canfield, J and Wells H. C. (1976) *100 Ways To Enhance Self-Esteem in the Classroom,* Prentice Hall: London.

Cooley, C H (1902) *Human Nature and Social Order.* Charles Scribners and Sons: New York.

Coombes, A (1985) 'Achieving Self-discipline: Some Basic Questions.' *Theory Into Practice,* Vol. XXIV No. 4.

Fountain, S (1990) *Learning Together,* W.W.F. and Stanley Thornes: Cheltenham.

Freed, A M (1971) *T.A. For Tots,* Jalmar Press.

Fuggitt, E (1973) *He Hit Me Back, First,* Jalmar Press.

Galloway, F (1989) *Personal And Social Education,* Pergamon Press: London.

Illsley-Clarke, J (1978) *Self-Esteem - A Family Affair,* Harper and Row: London.

Judson, S (1977) *A Manual on Non-violence and Children,* New Society Publishers.

Kreidler, W J (1984) *Creative Conflict Resolution,* Scott, Foresman.

Lawrence, D (1987) *Enhancing Self-Esteem in the Classroom,* PCP. Education Ltd.

Luce, R D and Raiffa, H (1957) *Games and Decisions,* Wiley: New York.

Masheder, M (1986) *Let's Co-operate,* Peace Education Project of Peace Pledge Union, 6, Endsleigh Street, London.

Masheder, M (1989) *Let's Play Together,* Green Print, The Merlin Press.

Miller, B and Miller, T (1990) *That's Not Fair!,* Pergamon Press Ltd: London.

Moreno, J L (1970) *'The Viennese Origins of the Encounter Movement Paving the Way for Existentialism, Group Therapy and Psychodrama,'* Group Psychotherapy, 22.

Mosley, J (1993) *Turn Your School Around,* LDA.

Nicholas, F M (1987) *Coping With Conflict,* LDA.

Orlick, T (1978) *The Co-operative Sports And Games Book,* Pantheon Publishers.

Pax Christi *Winners All,* Pax Christi, 9 Henry Road, London.

Palmer, P (1977) *Liking Myself,* Impact Publishers.

Pike, G and Selby, D (1988) *Global Teacher, Global Learner,* Hodder and Stoughton: London.

Prutzman, P (1987) *The Friendly Classroom For A Small Planet,* CCRC.

Rawlins, G and Rich, J (1985) *Look, Listen And Trust,* Nelson: London.

Satir, V (1975) *Self-Esteem,* Celestial Arts.

Steiner, C (1977) *The Original Warm Fuzzy Tale,* Jalmar Press.

Thacker, J (1984) *Project on Developmental Groupwork in Pastoral Care and Personal/Social Education in Junior and Middle Schools:* A Report of the First Year of the Project 1983/84, Unpublished report. Centre for Personal Social and Moral Education, School of Education University of Exeter.

Weinstein, M and Goodman, J (1980) *Playfair,* Impact Publishers.

White, M (1991) *Self-Esteem,* Daniels Publishing.

Woodcraft Folk (1989) *Games, Games, Games,* The Woodcraft Folk, 13 Ritherdon Rd., London.